The American
QUARTER HORSE
in Pictures

The

American
QUARTER HORSE
in Pictures

MARGARET CABELL SELF

Published by
Melvin Powers
WILSHIRE BOOK COMPANY
12015 Sherman Road
No. Hollywood, California 91605
Telephone: (213) 875-1711 / (818) 983-1105

Printed by

HAL LEIGHTON PRINTING COMPANY
P.O. Box 3952
North Hollywood, California 91605
Telephone: (818) 983-1105

Library of Congress Catalog Card Number 69-18637

Designed by William E. Lickfield

Manufactured in the United States of America
ISBN 0-87980-237-5

6906

Acknowledgments

I SHOULD like to thank all the people who were kind enough to send me pictures and other material for this book. Some went to endless trouble, hunting up unusual pictures, having special ones taken, and so forth. I would also like to thank Mr. Rex Cauble for his graciousness and cooperation in putting his facilities at my disposal and so making it possible for me to take the informal pictures of mares, foals, and early training and handling. But most of all I want to thank Mr. Garford Wilkinson of the American Quarter Horse Association for his patience in answering my questions, for getting me many pictures, and for supplying me with the material from which the paragraphs concerning the rules of the Association, the activities of the youth program, and the statistics on racing were taken.

MARGARET CABELL SELF

Contents

Part I

Origin and History

Eohippus, the Dawn Horse, the little, catlike, soft-toed, weaponless animal which roamed the Americas, so many eons ago, is the accepted ancestor of the modern equine race. Unlike the descendants of the great mastodon (father of the modern elephant) which resemble him to some extent and of which there are only a few distinct varieties, the descendants of Eohippus in no way resemble their forefather. Furthermore, today there are nearly a hundred distinct breeds of horses, each with its own particular conformation and use.

Two major factors contributed to the emergence of so many different types from one common ancestor: adaptation to a specific natural environment, and purposeful selection and breeding programs undertaken by man. As examples of the first, we have the thin-skinned, high-tailed, nervous little Arabian, whose physical characteristics enable him to survive in a hot climate, and the heavy-coated, close-tailed Mongolian pony of the steppes, whose big nasal passages enable the cold air to be warmed up before entering his lungs and whose teeth with their enormously long roots permit him to live on sticks and roots rather than on grass. As examples of how selective breeding can change the appearance and physical characteristics of a breed, we might contrast tremendous draft horses, such as the Belgians, suitable for slow work requiring bodily weight and strong muscles, with the peacock of the horse world, the gaited-saddler, with his delicate structure and extremely high action. As will be seen, both these factors contributed to the development of the American Quarter Horse.

Since very early days, man's interest in the sport of racing has moved him to breed horses suitable for that purpose. First came the English Thoroughbred. By crossing the small, sensitive, desert-bred Arabian, easily excited to flight, with the more phlegmatic, slower, but larger European mare, breeders produced an animal with the speed of the Arabian plus the longer legs of the larger mare and so developed a horse that could outrun either.

Later came the Standardbred or harness racer. This development occurred partly because early Blue Laws forbade ordinary racing in some states, partly also because—while the interest in flat racing for the ordinary man was in the betting—the farmer and the socialite, the one on his way to town driving his little Morgan and the other with his stylish rig, carriage, or sleigh, liked to challenge a neighbor to a friendly "brush" down the village street or along the snow-covered roads and so enjoy the excitement of driving his own stallion or mare in a race. In developing the Standardbred, breeders used stallions of Thoroughbred ancestry but chose those whose progeny had speed at the trot or at the pace, rather than at the gallop.

A still different type of racing was very popular in the eighteenth century, especially in the Tidewater section of Virginia. When the colonists first moved into this territory they found there a breed of small horse known as "Chickasaws" running wild in the great forests. Since the Spanish Conquistadors had brought the first modern horses to the New World, these animals, like the Mustangs of the western plains must have been descendants of the Spanish horses and so can also be traced back to the desert Arabian. Because of inbreeding, lack of forage in winter, and so on, these animals had been reduced in size until they were really ponies. They had developed a hide thick enough to withstand the flies. Above all, they had learned to be ever alert for the predatory mountain lion and to fly off like the wind at his approach.

As the colonists settled in and began to clear the land prior to growing tobacco and cotton, they began to import blooded horses for pleasure and sport. Ordinary racing was denied them—there were no race tracks or even open roads of any appreciable length or straightness—so they invented a new type of race. They cleared two parallel paths through the forest, from six to twelve feet in width and separated from each other by uncleared land. Two horses only raced at a time, one on each path. The length of these paths was about a quarter of a mile, hence the name "quarter race" or "quarter racing." The colonists soon discovered that the horse most suited to this kind of racing, which required no staying power but only the ability to start fast, stop fast, and go at top speed for a very brief period, was neither the little native Chickasaw, which was too small and weedy to carry a full-grown man at speed, nor yet the long-legged Thoroughbred, but rather the progeny which resulted when a Thoroughbred stallion was put to a Chickasaw mare.

And so the Quarter Horse, the horse that could run fast "as long as he could hold his breath," a result both of adaptation to natural environment and of man's desire to amuse himself, came into being.

One of the three Foundation Sires of the English Thoroughbred was the Godolphin Arabian or, more correctly, the Godolphin Barb. He sired a race horse called English Janus, which in turn sired a horse named Little Janus. As his name indicates, Little Janus was small in stature, being certainly not over 14:2 hands. He was a bright chestnut, very compact and well formed, but his muscles were quite different in character from those of the ordinary race horse. Instead of being long and flat they were bunchy and bulging. He had tremendous heart and, in spite of his short legs, was speedy enough to race successfully and win in at least two of the grueling 4 four-mile heat races of his day.

A strained sinew early in his career retired him to the stud of an Anthony Langley Swymmer, under whose colors he had raced. Some time in the latter 1750's he became the property of Mordecai Booth of Gloucester, Virginia, who had him brought to the New World.

He had served in Eastern Virginia for four years when, his sinew having healed, he went back to racing. Meanwhile it developed that Janus was a most unusual stallion and an exceedingly prepotent one. One reason why Arabian blood has been used so extensively to improve many other breeds of horses is that the infusion of this blood not only introduces Arabian characteristics to the get but seems to bring out and improve the best characteristics of the original stock. And so it was with Janus. When he was put to Thoroughbred mares, the result was progeny that made wonderful records on the regular tracks, running the four-mile heats without tiring. When he was put to the little native Chickasaws, the ability to start, stop, and turn quickly and to run short distances at speed were improved outstandingly in the progeny. There were probably fewer stallions of pure blood that could pass on exactly these characteristics than there were of the ordinary Thoroughbred type, so as the country opened up and ordinary racing became popular, Janus was moved farther west to Roanoke, Virginia, where he served mares from around that district and from North Carolina for many years, propagating a particularly speedy, hardy, good-looking line of Quarter Horses.

THE
QUARTER HORSE
MOVES
WESTWARD

After the American Revolution, with the opening up of all of the eastern seaboard and with the growth of large plantations all over the South, the interest in quarter racing in those localities declined, to be superseded by organized flat racing, steeple chasing, and hunting. Cotton and tobacco were the big crops, and only work horses were required to produce them. As for pleasure horses, when the plantation owner was not out on his Thoroughbred, hunting the fox, he was driving or riding his high-stepping Saddler, forerunner of the fine-harness horse, whose delightful gaits and spirited carriage made him the envy of all. Farther south the less affluent plantation owners not so interested in style were to develop a different type of saddle horse, the "Plantation Walker," which carried his owner at a fast running walk, easy on the bones, or at a comfortable, rocking-chair canter between the rows of tobacco. It seemed as though the speedy little Quarter Horse might easily disappear from the scene.

Fortunately, this was the time of the great pioneer movement to the West. And, equally fortunately, with the pioneers went the Quarter Horse, not just to provide sport and amusement but as a mainstay of the economy. For in the West cattle rather than cotton and corn was the main crop, and for running cattle a sturdy, intelligent, swift, hardy, and active horse is a necessity. To be sure there were the wild mustangs, similar in ancestry to the Chickasaws. But, as plantation owners had previously discovered, the wild horses were neither big enough nor fleet enough to do the work at hand. They needed the infusion of outside bloodlines to improve their natural abilities, increase their stature, and thus produce the ideal stock horse. Thoroughbred, Standardbred, Saddler, and Morgan bloodlines were all introduced, but in the end Quarter Horse stallions or those with Quarter Horse characteristics were found to be the most successful. And so the little quarter racer found his true vocation and came into his own.

Three outstanding stallions stand out in the pages of equine history as being the most important in the development of the Quarter Horse at this time. The first is Copperbottom (1828–1860); he was the son of the Thoroughbred Sir Archy and, through his dam, traced back to Janus. The second was another descendant of Sir Archy named Shiloh (1840–1869). Finally and most popular of all came Steel Dust (1845–1874). So many were the claimants for Steel Dust ancestry that the name is almost synonymous with the term "stock horse!"

The mating of Shiloh to a daughter of Steel Dust produced another fine and prepotent sire, with the plain name of Billy (1860–1886). The family that Billy founded figures in the pedigree of many modern Quarter Horses. Billy and Steel Dust were among the first to stand in the state of Texas.

One of the most active breeders interested primarily in improving the stock horse was Captain Richard King, who founded the King Ranch in Texas. King began by mating the native horses with imported Thoroughbreds. This was successful to some extent, since it improved the fineness of the native animal and increased its size, but—as the Klebergs, who took over the King Ranch after the Captain's death, found—that though the first and second cross showed good results without diminishing the desirable characteristics of the native horse, too much Thoroughbred blood produced horses that were too nervous to work cattle successfully, too delicate and thin-skinned to live off the country, too leggy, and too prone to sprains and strains to negotiate the sudden stops, starts, and turns that are necessary. The time had come to find another sire, preferably of Quarter Horse strain, and with his help produce the ideal stock horse. In 1916 they bought an animal of Quarter Horse breeding called Old Sorrel. He proved to be the finest cow horse they had ever owned.

With hopes that he would be able to pass along his sagacity and ability to future generations, they bred him as a start to fifty of their best working mares, all with at least a quarter Thoroughbred blood and many with half. An outstanding son, Solis, was then mated to one of Old Sorrel's daughters; the result was most gratifying, and the experiment was continued by mating Solis to forty of his halfsisters, most or all of whom were from the same band of halfbred and quarterbred mares.

BREEDING
ACTIVITIES
AT THE
KING RANCH

Of all the sons of Old Sorrel, Solis proved most prepotent and was the only one with sufficiently strong genes to stand up under the program of line and close inbreeding that was undertaken in order to perpetuate the blood of Old Sorrel. The most outstanding son of Solis is Wimpy, P-1.

WIMPY, P-1

Wimpy is known to all as the foremost and first foundation sire of the modern American Quarter Horse, for it was he that was chosen to receive the registration number 1 when the American Quarter Horse Association was formed. His portrait is a fitting frontispiece for this book.

THE
AMERICAN
QUARTER HORSE
ASSOCIATION

For many years after the Quarter Horse became standardized as to type and preferred bloodlines were recognized, there was no attempt to form an association that would register qualified members of the breed. Cattlemen were mostly interested in their horses as working animals. While the great horses of the past were known and referred to, the tremendous current interest in showing had not yet developed.

In 1938 the Texas Palomino Association was formed for the purpose of promoting and registering Palomino horses. Since this is a color breed, not one descended from one type of horse or of horses of one particular bloodline, it included horses of many different kinds. However, the horse in which this "golden" coloring most often appeared was the Quarter Horse, and many Quarter Horses were registered in the Palomino book.

In 1939 several preliminary meetings were held by members of the Palomino Association who were also vitally interested in Quarter Horses as a breed and who wanted to form an association of their own. Among these were Roy Davis, later to become editor of the *Quarter Horse Journal*, Professor Robert Denhardt of Texas A & M University, and R. L. Underwood of Wichita Falls. These discussions led to a larger meeting held at Fort Worth in March of 1940, which seventy-five attended. It was at this meeting that the American Quarter Horse Association was formed with the declared purposes of collecting and recording pedigrees, publishing a stud book and registry, and doing all it could to promote, improve, and publicize the Quarter Horse. An initial offering of eight hundred shares of stock was immediately offered and oversubscribed. The AQHA was on its way.

The headquarters of the AMERICAN QUARTER HORSE ASSOCIATION is located in Amarillo, Texas. In 1968 the AQHA completed a $600,000 expansion of their already large and beautiful building. Here are housed the executives and staff of the AQHA, of the *Quarter Horse Journal,* and of the Quarter Horse Racing Commission.

Through 1968 the Association registered a total of 573,832 animals. Thus the AQHA has registered more animals than any other breeding association, including the Jockey Club.

The Registration Department, of course, is perhaps the most important department of the AQHA. In an enormous file room are folders for every horse with a numbered certificate. No horse may be shown in an approved Quarter Horse show without such a certificate, nor may he race on a Quarter Horse track. It should be noted that the rules concerning the registrations of Quarter Horses and the awarding of numbers underwent a change in 1962. Prior to that time the American Quarter Horse Association awarded two types of numbers, numbered registrations, awarded to horses of pure Quarter Horse bloodlines, and appendix certificates. Thus WIMPY, 1, had a permanent registration number with

Association policies are formed through a Board of Directors, one from each of the fifty states and from Canada. The directors annually elect an Executive Committee and an Executive Secretary. The Executive Committee for 1969 was (seated, from left) Jay Pumphrey, Lee Berwick, Bill Verdugo, and (standing) A. H. Ferber, Jr., Bill Thompson, Don Jones.

In the computer room, a battery of electronic computers can show the breeding, ownership, performance, and racing records of any registered animal in a matter of minutes.

the AQHA. Horses in the appendix could be advanced by obtaining a Register of Merit, by passing conformation inspection, and through produce of dam and get of sire. These horses with appendix listings then could compete in all shows and contests, including racing.

Since January 1, 1962, stallions, mares, and geldings foaled in 1962 or after are eligible for registry as follows: If they have a numbered Quarter Horse sire and a numbered Quarter Horse dam, they receive a registration number in the official stud book, with no inspection con-

Garford Wilkinson is head of Public Relations. Questions and correspondence regarding the AQHA should be directed to him.

formation. If they have one numbered Quarter Horse parent and one parent registered with the Jockey Club, they are registered in the New Appendix; at any time after two years of age such a horse is eligible for advancement by qualifying for one of the Registers of Merit and then passing conformation inspection. Those which so qualify are then registered in the official stud book and receive a number.

Other departments include the carding section, where markings of the horse are drawn on the registration of each horse and reference files on get or progeny of all registered Quarter Horses are maintained, and depart-

The *Quarter Horse Journal,* a splendid publication, is edited by Roy Davis, who was one of the original sponsors of the AQHA.

Courtesy of the American Quarter Horse Association.

ments to handle transfer records, data processing, and accounting, as well as Public Relations and Public Information.

Performance classes take in all except halter classes in approved Quarter Horse shows. In 1968 there were 1,416 approved shows in which 39,440 horses competed. Horses winning in all types of classes receive points. A complete record of these points is kept, and from this record are awarded the AQHA Championships and Registers of Merit Certificates.

The Youth Activities Program not only approves shows limited to junior exhibitors, as well as classes in all shows for them (for which it provides handsome trophies), but includes an extension service, which offers advice to directors of 4-H clubs, provides lists of approved judges, and publishes a film list and many excellent brochures, which may be had on request. Part V discusses the Youth Activities Program in greater detail.

No discussion of the activities of the American Quarter Horse Association would be complete without mentioning the aid that it gives to equine research programs now in progress at several state universities and research centers. It has donated upwards of a half-million dollars to promote the welfare of all horses, since this work was started in 1960, and has made available an index of current equine research activities which is available at the Morris Animal Foundation, 531 Guaranty Bank Building, Denver, Colorado.

There are more than 150 local, state, and regional Quarter Horse associations in this and other countries, with Mexico and Canada among the most active of the foreign affiliations. In all there are about 40,000 dues paying members.

Part II

The Quarter Horse Today

There are certain basic physical "beauties" desirable in all horses. These include a well-proportioned head set correctly on a neck that is neither too thick nor too willowy; a reasonably sloping shoulder topped by withers that are neither so flat and thick as to be termed "mutton withers" nor extremely high and knifelike. The legs of the working horse should be set on straight and should appear so when looked at from the front, side, or rear. Short cannons and short backs make for strength, and length from croup to buttock point provides haunches of great power and, therefore, both speed and the ability to stop, start, and turn quickly. Depth of heart and a good barrel give enough room to house the internal organs. Seen as a whole, the horse of any breed should present an attractive, harmonious picture rather than the appearance of being a composite of several animals, with a head too heavy for his neck or a back too long for the length of his legs.

In addition to these basically good physical "points," there are specifications for each horse of a certain breed as to "points" which improve his performance and appearance as a horse of that particular breed. The special qualifications relating to the Quarter Horse are as follows:

No absolute minimum or maximum requirements for weight and height are given in the registration rules, but the generally accepted measurements are 14:3 to 15:1 hands and 1,100 to 1,300 pounds. It will be noted that because of his surprisingly heavy muscular development the Quarter Horse is far heavier for his height than are the Thoroughbred, Standardbred, or Saddlebred horses.

The following body colors are acceptable for registration of Quaker Horses: bay, black, brown, sorrel, chestnut, dun, buckskin, red dun, grullo (mouse colored), palomino, gray, red roan, blue roan. He may have white

PHYSICAL
CHARACTERISTICS

Height and Weight

Colors and Markings

markings on head or legs and an occasional small spot of white on the body, but horses with white markings resembling those on pintos, horses with appaloosa markings, and albino horses are not permitted to be registered in the Quarter Horse Book.

Head

The ideal head of the Quarter Horse is comparatively small. A slightly concave (dished) profile is desirable though not necessary. A Roman nose or convex profile would be penalized. As with all breeds the ears should be fine, well set, and alert, since they indicate sensitivity and intelligence. The eyes should be fairly wide apart and they, too, should be alert and wide awake, not mean or sleepy looking. The outstanding characteristic of the head of the Quarter Horse which sets it apart from the ideal type of head for other breeds is the surprisingly well-developed muscle of the jaw. When viewed from behind this muscle is rounded, giving a strong appearance to the cheek not seen in other breeds.

Neck and Throttle

The neck of the Quarter Horse should be slightly crested and moderately thick, but these characteristics should not be exaggerated. His throttle should be well cut out and sufficiently wide to allow the horse to breathe easily in running, but, again, this line should not be overly wide or open.

Profile of a champion, CUTTER BILL, P-53,703.

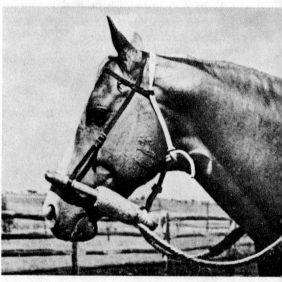

Photo by Margaret Cabell Se

Courtesy of Bob and Bonnie Hembrook, Cackleberry Ranch. Photo by Dalco Film Co.

WHAT A BONANZA, 322,283, is an AQHA Grand Champion. He has been shown as Halter Stallion in twenty states and has been named Grand Champion Stallion sixty-one times and Reserve Champion Stallion thirty-two times, accumulating 245 points in halter classes. He is by Coy's Bonanza, 134,099, by Jaquar, 46,483. His dam is Tooter Kay, 50,044, by King Black, 18,569.

The chest of the Quarter Horse should be wide, when seen from the front, and his forelegs set well apart. Seen from the side the chest should be very deep from withers to girth line. The muscling of arm and forearm is well defined, much more so than in other breeds, denoting tremendous strength and explaining the ability of this horse to carry his weight on his forehand, most of the time, without injuring himself.

Front

As in all breeds a sloping shoulder sweeping back to a moderately prominent wither is desirable. The shoulders of the Quarter Horse have more strongly defined muscles than those of other horses, in keeping with the

Shoulders, Croup, and Withers

[27]

OTOE, P-128,989, is one of the most outstanding stallions in the country. As a sire his progeny, both fillies and colts, were winners in the 1965 American Royal. Joy, one of his fillies, was shown twenty times, being placed first each time in such shows as Oklahoma State Fair, Texas State Fair, and American Royal. Hard to Beat, a stallion sired by Otoe, has placed as High Point Stallion of the nation. In his own right Otoe has been many times Grand Champion Show Horse at such shows as Fort Worth, International at Chicago, and Pan-American Exposition. As a race horse he gained his rating of AAA as well as AQHA Champion early in the year he was two, the only horse ever to do so. His breeding is straight Quarter Horse except for one grandsire, Three Bars, that was a Thoroughbred.

Courtesy of Becky Allen.

Hindquarters

rest of his conformation. Withers and croup should be on a line with one another.

The hindquarters of the Quarter Horse, running from the point of the croup down to the hocks, are his most outstanding physical characteristic. So true is this that the majority of the pictures of Quarter Horses used in sales advertisements are taken from the rear. (This has led some people to think erroneously that the horse acquired his name because of outstanding muscular development in this part of his body.) The croup should be sloping, rather than level, and the tail not held away from the body. It should appear wide as seen from behind, and the outline of the muscles in the areas of the thigh, stifle, and gaskin should be well defined. The stifle itself extends out below the hip so that, seen from behind, this is the widest part of the horse.

Muscular Development and Center of Gravity

It must be reiterated that the two things which are responsible for the speed and handiness of the Quarter Horse are his thick, bulgy, extremely powerful muscles

[28]

JOE CODY, P-42,543, is an AQHA champion, winning his points in cutting, roping, and reining classes as well as in halter classes. He has sired many AQHA champions and at least two World Champions, Easter Cody and Sappho Cody. His sire was Bill Cody, P-3244, by Wimpy, P-1; his dam: Taboo, P-7073; by King, P-234. Joe Cody's conformation and muscular development speak for themselves.

Courtesy of Willow Brook Farms and C. T. Fuller. Photo by Mr. Fuller.

and the relationship of his center of gravity (much farther to the front than in other breeds) and angle of thrust to stride. The natural way for a Quarter Horse to stand or move with or without a rider is with his weight on his forehand. This reduces the angle of thrust, making for less elevation and more speed. It also makes him tire easily, but since in racing over short courses and working as a cow horse only short spurts of speed are required, this is not a handicap.

Since the value of the Quarter Horse lies in his speed, exaggeratedly high action would not be desirable. He should travel true with no signs of brushing or interfering. His feet should be placed flat as he moves, neither toe first nor heel first; the former makes for stumblers, the latter for instability on slippery surfaces. At the walk his hind legs should reach well under him. In competition he may be required to stop and turn with his hindquarters so far under him that his hocks almost touch the ground; this is true in cutting horse classes, for example.

ACTION

BLAZE WAGON, 319,997, AQHA Champion stallion, has a Register of Merit in Reining and one in Pleasure. He displays good shoulder development and head carriage, though the curve of the throttle is somewhat wider than is usual and his croup seems higher than the point of the withers.

Courtesy of Bob and Lila Lee.

CUE BALL STAR, 105,242, a sorrel stallion, was foaled in 1959 in California. By Star Lighter out of Peachie Cue Ball, he is a Pacific Coast Quarter Horse Association Futurity winner and Grand Champion many times. His owner writes that he has an ideal disposition.

Amiability and the desire to cooperate are well demonstrated here, at the opening of a new furniture plant of the Huntingburg Furniture Company. It seemed appropriate, for the ceremony of cutting the ribbon, for a cutting horse to officiate, especially since his name was CUTTER BILL, Mr. Rex Cauble, owner of the gentle stallion, is holding him while Board Chairman Harold McCurtrie and President Joe C. Wulfman stand by.

Courtesy of the Cauble Ranch.

On the other hand he may sometimes be asked to turn with his body curved to the circle and his weight slightly over his center or on the forehand, as in executing figures of eight and circles in reining competitions.

The Quarter Horse is an extremely sensible, tractable and willing animal without being nervous. He has the speed of the hot-blooded horses of his ancestry without their tendency to hysteria; the stability of the cold-blooded horses without their stubbornness. In addition he has a high degree of intelligence. His training has taught him not to rely on commands from his rider when exhibiting his ability as a Cutting Horse but to follow the movements of the calf or steer and make his own decisions as to where and when to turn. This "cow sense" is not highly developed in all Quarter Horses, and those that do not have it earn their living doing something other than working cattle.

The Quarter Horse is an extremely obedient horse, easily trained to stand without tying, to keep tension on a rope while the dismounted rider runs to tie up the calf, and so forth. Yet he gives an expert rider a good ride. Above all, he is an honest horse, giving all he has in his work.

As with the Morgan, the Quarter Horse often lives to a ripe and useful old age. Horses still active in their late twenties are not rare, and they often go on into their thirties.

TEMPERAMENT

This is SILVER KING, foaled in 1937, who in 1968 was one of three living sons of Old Sorrel. The latter, foaled in 1914, sired Silver King at the age of twenty-three. Silver King himself was still serving at twenty-six and was only retired so that he might live to a ripe old age with no duties other than passing his last days in peace and contentment.

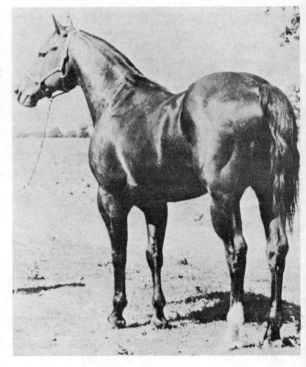

Part III

Breeding and Training Programs

The most important character at any breeding establishment is the stallion. He must have outstanding conformation and a desirable disposition, and he must have been proven to be prepotent by the records of his get. Preferably he will have a show record of his own in performance as well as halter classes.

Courtesy of the Cauble Ranch.

CUTTER BILL, P-53,703, amply fulfills these requirements. A palomino stallion, height 14:3, weight 1,175 pounds, he is head stud horse at the ranch of Rex C. Cauble. He is by Buddy Dexter, P-16,341, out of Billie Silvertone, P-574. The sire was Dexter, P-193, and the dam's sire Silvertone, P-190. Cutter Bill was AQHA Junior Registered Cutting Horse in 1959. In 1962 he was judged World's Champion Cutting Horse and World's Champion Cutting Horse Stallion by the National Cutting Horse Association, was on the AQHA Honor Roll as a cutting horse, and set a new World's Champion record for monies won in any one year.

In 1963, Cutter Bill again earned the requisite points for a world championship in the NCHA records as Cutting Horse Stallion and as Reserve World Champion Cutting Horse, and winner of the Tournament of Champions held in Little Rock, Arkansas. Finally, as proof of his prepotency, he is the only World Champion Cutting Horse to sire a World Champion Cutting Horse and also to sire a World Champion Halter Horse.

Routines at the Cauble Ranch

The next sixteen pictures were taken by the author on the Cauble Ranch in Texas with the kind cooperation of the owner. They show something of how a breeding program at one modern ranch is carried on.

Mares and foals are brought in from pasture each morning and put in a small, high-fenced corral.

A tease stallion is also brought in, and the mares are allowed to approach him at will. Those showing interest are then separated from the rest. Later in the morning they will meet with Cutter Bill or one of the other studs standing at the Cauble Ranch.

A second reason for this daily routine is that it gives the men an opportunity to check the mares and foals for possible injuries incurred in the pasture and for indispositions. Furthermore, the youngsters become used to being handled and so do not fear mankind. Here one of the men, carrying a pail of disinfectant, holds his hand out to a foal showing signs of scours.

The diagnosis having proved correct, one of the other men, rope over shoulder, herds mare and foal over to the fence. While the mare stands nearby, the foal will be treated and then allowed to return to the herd.

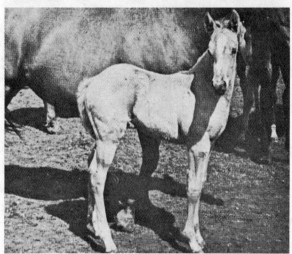

Another youngster watches the procedure but shows no fear.

Mr. Cauble takes a great interest in accustoming the young stock to being handled. He holds out his hand to a very new baby, but this one is still a little shy.

A bolder and slightly older bay foal comes up of his own accord and allows Mr. Cauble to lift up his front foot.

Seeing that no harm has come to his playmate, the first foal comes near enough to have his lips and muzzle stroked, while the little bay, with Mr. Cauble's arm resting on his rump, nibbles contentedly at the latter's coat.

Inspection over, the mares and foals are turned back out to pasture.

The ranch has several natural ponds which provide fresh water. On leaving the inspection paddock, one mare makes directly for one of these. . .

. . . while another stops on the top of a knoll to graze. Like human children, young foals stay close to their mothers at first. But as they grow older they sometimes go visiting. The three-week-old bay and dun foals have come over to make the acquaintance of the younger sorrel foal in the center.

This does not please the mare, who thinks her baby is too young for company. She moves quietly off, knowing he will follow, which he does as soon as he realizes that she has left him. As he canters after her, head up and ears pricked, the little dun follows along to keep him company.

On a nearby knoll, another young foal takes a siesta while his mother grazes close by. He exemplifies the Spanish proverb which says, "How pleasant it is to do nothing and, having done nothing, to rest!"

Yearling fillies in a nearby pasture also have nothing to do but enjoy themselves. They, too, are handled and inspected from time to time, but no formal training is given them.

As we approach a few heads are raised, but there is no sign of fear. So accustomed to mankind are they that they have lost the young foal's curiosity and just continue placidly to eat—a far cry from earlier times, when young stock associated man only with a painful experience with the branding iron.

In about six months this shaggy young lady will be brought into the barn, where careful grooming will rid her of the last vestiges of her yearling coat. If it is decided that she will be kept to be trained as a cutting horse, she will be halter broken and trained to walk, trot, and canter alongside a mounted rider.

Mr. Cauble, like the Quarter Horse breeders of earlier times, is also interested in improving his stock by introducing Thoroughbred blood. He is shown here stroking a yearling sired by Cutter Bill out of a Thoroughbred mare.

Photo by Joe Brown.

HANDLING AND BASIC TRAINING

When tremendous bands of wild horses roamed the western plains and could be had for the catching, when no particular attention was being paid to selective breeding, and when labor was cheap and the supply of cowhands unlimited, it was the custom to handle very young stock only once, when they were rounded up and branded. After that experience, the colt returned to the wilderness for another three or four years. Then, if he looked as though he would make a good cow horse, he was herded into a corral with his fellows. One by one each wild-eyed, terrified youngster was roped, thrown, saddled, and mounted. He was then encouraged to buck so that he would learn the hard way that it did no good, that there was no way to avoid the punishment of bit and

[41]

spur except by submitting. Perhaps there were a few legs broken, either men's or horses', but there were plenty more of both as replacements. Certainly there were plenty of spirited, intelligent animals that under this treatment became outlaws fit only for bronc riding at the rodeos. Under a different system they would have made excellent cow horses.

The American Indian, usually associated in most people's minds with cruelty, had a gentler approach. To him a horse was greatly to be valued, never to be risked unnecessarily. Every tribe had its official horsebreakers. When a band of wild horses was spotted that included some worthwhile animals, it was slowly maneuvered into a gorge or other natural pen. At the same time, the Indians gradually accustomed the horses to their presence, until they could come within a few hundred feet and even make unusual noises without disturbing them.

Once in the gorge, a desired horse was gently separated from the herd, and the horsebreaker began his work. Carrying a small blanket and a little noose of woven horsehair only a half inch in diameter, and taking perhaps an hour to approach, he would finally slip the noose over the horse's head. There is a certain spot in the area of the nasal bones where, if pressure is applied, the nerve is so affected that the horse cannot fight. With the noose so placed that it pressed on this point, the pressure would gradually be relaxed, to be tightened only if the horse moved. It took but a short time for the horse to associate pain with movement and a willingness to stand with the reward of freedom from pain.

This lesson learned, and with the noose in place but loose, the horsebreaker would run his hands all over the horse's body, keeping up a constant murmuring or low whistling. Frightened at first the horse would finally grow so calm that he would allow the man to touch even sensitive parts such as the ears without moving. At first the handling would be gentle. Then the man would slap the horse, first lightly, then harder, until he became accustomed to this also. Finally, picking up his little blanket, the Indian would let the horse smell it; he would rub him with it; he would wave it around him. At last he would slap him with it, still without hurting the animal, to show him there was nothing to fear.

Perhaps after a day's handling, the horse would no longer be afraid of the man. He could even be mounted and moved about the improvised corral, though it would take more patience to teach him to react to shifts of weight and the pressure of moccasined feet. The horse would never know the feel of rowel or bit; these were not necessary, for the horse was governed by a man who had become half horse himself. The two were one.

Good horses today are not picked up for nothing. They cost money—a good deal of money. Perhaps horses destined just for ranch work are still being broken by the old methods, but not so with horses that are expected to bring a high price in the sales ring and that have the blood of champions in their veins. The following pictures are presented through the courtesy of the American Quarter Horse Association. The first nine were taken at the King Ranch.

Where the foals are handled daily, they do not need to be approached as shown here, but if they are shy it may be necessary. We see two men, having herded a young foal into a corner, approach him quietly, a hand held out to show friendship.

The corner forms a barricade which he cannot evade. The men, together, form another, and for a moment he is crowded until a light head stall can be slipped on.

The men step back; one strokes the youngster's haunch, the other his neck. The colt is unafraid.

The halter may be of soft leather, or it may be a homemade hackamore of soft rope.

The next step is to get the colt used to having first a front foot. . .

and then a hind foot lifted and stroked. As in the Indian method, the whole purpose of this handling is to teach the colt that man is not to be feared.

One of several approaches to teaching the weanling that a tug on the hackamore means to go forward. By means of a short rope he is attached to a female burro. The burro is calm, exceedingly strong, and considerably heavier than the weanling. He soon learns to stay with her wherever she goes.

Some trainers prefer this method. A soft, light rope is run around the haunches of the foal. The trainer holds this in one hand, along with the lead shank. In the other hand he carries a lead fastened to the halter of the foal's mother. He then leads the two together. If the foal pulls back he can urge him along by tightening the rope that encircles the haunches.

[45]

When the youngster has learned the meaning of the tug on the hackamore and the pressure of the haunch rope, the trainer can lead him alone without the mare. This method is generally used in stables throughout the world to teach foals to lead without battling them and frightening them.

This is the extent of training for the weanling. He will now be allowed to return to his fellows. In some establishments he will be handled very little until the time comes for more serious training. In others he will be kept near the barn, brought in frequently for inspection and feeding, and, through constant handling, never allowed to forget that man is both friend and master.

At the Cauble Ranch the two-year-olds selected to be kept and trained are brought into the barn and introduced to the daily routine of being thoroughly groomed. Having been handled since birth, they soon become accustomed to it. This is Billy Frost, an appealing youngster.

They are introduced to the "horsewalker." This was constructed on the ranch from pipes.

Courtesy of the Cauble Ranch. Photo by the author.

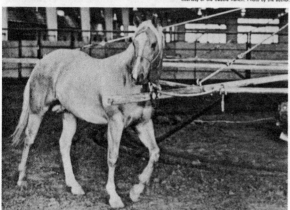

A motor turns the walker. Note that for safety the horse is fastened by a short chain and by a rope shank. The worst thing that could happen at this stage would be for a horse to find out that it is possible for him to break loose.

Photo by the author.

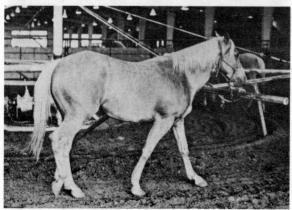

If the colt has had his morning exercise he can be walked cool. If the walker is to be used for an hour of exercise, it can be speeded up so that the colts work at a jog. It can also be reversed. Here Bill's Pat is cooling out. Notice the poles arranged to drag along the ground. Should a youngster try to pull back, these dig into the ground and act as brakes.

Photo by the author.

[47]

Young animals that are constantly handled usually have no fear the first time something strange is put on their backs. But those turned out after their early handling days may be more timid.

Courtesy AQHA

On the King Ranch, we see "sacking out." A bag is suspended on each side of the young animal and he is led around to accustom him to the feeling.

Courtesy AQHA

That lesson learned, two men quietly introduce him to the saddle . . . after which he may be turned loose in the corral to buck and play and learn for himself that there is no way for him to shake it off.

Courtesy AQHA

The trainer will also make a practice of leading him in his new attire while mounted on another horse. The young horse becomes accustomed not only to the feel of the unusual equipment but to the noise of flapping leather and jingling spur.

Courtesy AHQA

Several more lessons are taught; in different establishments they are introduced in a different sequence. Among them is the first experience with a bit. There are several types to choose from. One is the ordinary snaffle with a loose, dangling object (called "keys") attached to it. The other consists of a complete circle with loops for attaching it to the head stall. The keys hang in the mouth and dangle against the tongue; the lower half of the circle goes under the jaw. The purpose of both these bits is to teach the horse to learn to play with the keys. As he snatches at them he bends his poll and relaxes his jaw. Sometimes a coating of molasses is used the first few times to make them pleasant to taste. In many stables the colt being "mouthed" in this fashion is backed into a standing stall. His halter is attached by shanks to each side which allow him plenty of freedom of the head, and he is left to stand and play with the mouthing bit for an hour or so each day.

(Left) A snaffle bit with keys. (Right) A ring bit, with keys here inverted.

Courtesy AHQA

Before being mounted, many trainers consider it wise to accustom the young horse to obeying voice commands. For this they use what is called a "longe" (pronounced *lunge*) line and a long training whip. The trainer stands in the center and keeps turning with the horse. The longe line controls the colt's forward motion; the whip, lightly held and waved from behind, urges him to increase his gait when this is desired. In a very short time under the hands of a skillful trainer the colt can be taught to circle around him at the walk, trot, or canter, as commanded, and to start, reverse, stop, and stand quietly at a word.

Longeing is generally started before the horse has been introduced to the saddle, but it is continued even after that lesson has been learned. This horse at the King Ranch is being exercised on the longe.

Courtesy AHQA

On a quiet morning, after an hour or more of being trotted beside a companion, the horse is mounted for the first time. He is unafraid; he has learned his lesson.

Courtesy AHQA

He still has to learn to bend at the poll instead of sticking his head up and his nose out; and to turn or circle on command will only be introduced very gradually. However, his kindergarten days may now be considered over.

Courtesy AHQA

Before describing the advanced training of the Quarter Horse, it would be well to explain why we have two different types of riding, Western riding and so-called English riding, and what the basic differences between them are. Then we can discuss the methods used to train a horse for either one purpose or the other.

Western riding was developed for the purpose of using the horse as an assistant to man in working cattle and in performing various chores around the ranch. Certain skills were encouraged and trained into the horse. Certain natural characteristics and aptitudes were looked for, and horses showing these were those chosen for training and breeding.

Among the skills and natural talents which the vaquero wants in a horse are: (1) the intelligence to work on his own, on a loose rein, thus leaving the man free to concentrate on the job he is doing; (2) the ability to come to a sliding stop, pivot quickly on the hindquarters with the haunches well under and start off again equally abruptly, and the ability to balance and turn sharply of his own accord to fit his movements to those of the animal he is pursuing or cutting out; (3) the ability to live off the land without requiring too much in the way of care. (A man working a large herd of cattle can't take the time to cool a horse out thoroughly and brush him down every time he rides him, and he does not want a horse with such a tender hide that flies bother him unduly.)

ADVANCED TRAINING: WESTERN AND ENGLISH

English training has a much longer history. As far back as 1400 B.C., an emperor of the Hittites had instructions engraved on stone tablets for the use of his stable manager in caring for his chariot horses. Bas-reliefs made by Philias around 350 B.C. show the horse carrying a rider and executing a number of movements that appear very strange to us. They are not strange, however, if we realize that these movements served the rider in hand-to-hand mounted combat.

The most important use for the horse until gunpowder was invented was in warfare. In early and medieval times, combat was virtually all hand-to-hand; later, as in the charge of the Light Brigade, the horses became a machine of many parts, all under the command of a leader and all having to move and turn with great precision.

In primeval times the horse had no weapons of defense. His basic nature—his innate timidity and his instinct to flee when frightened—would seem to make him unfit to be used on the battlefield, yet he has been used successfully there for a great many centuries. The reason man has been able to so use him is that as long ago as the days of the Greeks, men discovered that with a certain kind of training they could teach a horse to rely completely on his rider, taking his commands from him and making not the least movement without receiving such commands.

It is easy now to see why the horse developed for ranch work and the horse trained for English riding require completely different training. The vaquero teaches his horse to go on a completely loose rein and to work as much as possible on his own. The movements that he is taught to make are comparatively few in number, and their execution must be governed by the horse himself; there is no time for communication from the rider, since certain of them require an extraordinary balance which only the horse can know how to execute.

The horseman of the Middle Ages taught his horse movements which might save his life if he found himself in a tight corner. These movements—such as the levade, the corbette, the capriole—are so difficult that today they are taught in only a few places, such as in Austria at the Spanish Riding School of Vienna, but at one time they were commonplace in the education of all horses.

There were two weapons in common use for hand-to-hand fighting: the sword and the spear. To use either the rider needed a moment in which to aim and he needed to be so positioned that he could use his weapon effectively, so the war horse was taught to assume a position known as the "levade." Being at a halt he settled back on his hocks and raised his forehand off the ground with the forelegs relaxed. (Being as far back on the hocks as he would be if he had just come to a sliding stop, his croup and haunches were thus considerably lower than his forehand.) He would keep this position until told by the rider to return to a more normal one. It is easy to see how much more readily the knight, made awkward by his heavy armor, could use his long unwieldy spear when mounted on an animal so trained. But imagine the tremendous strength in the hindquarters and the perfect sense of balance that the horse had to develop in order to take and hold such an artificial position when carrying a heavily armored rider! And imagine how completely disciplined he must have been to execute this movement in the melee of battle while being threatened from all sides!

But this was by no means the extent of his training. Suppose that our medieval rider found himself outnumbered and entirely surrounded by the enemy, some mounted and some on foot and all pressing him hard. He must flee, but how to do so presented a problem. From the position of the levade he would tell his horse, through his aids, to rear, thus raising him in height above the enemy. While in the rearing position he would then cause him to take a few hopping steps forward (the corbette), thus clearing a space in front of him. On command the horse would then come down on all fours, immediately to spring straight up with an enormous leap. Exactly at the height of this bound he would kick back, extending his back legs until he seemed to be flying. This is the beautiful and hardly to be believed movement called the "capriole." By means of this maneuver the horse could clear a considerable space behind him. As he landed the rider again would communicate his wishes and the horse would pirouette on his hindquarters and depart at the gallop, carrying his rider to safety.

Needless to say, the trainer did not start the education of the horse with these advanced movements. First he had to teach him to understand the language of the aids and to obey their commands. Then he had to introduce a series of exercises, some quite simple, such as circling and turning (but done in a precise way with the horse's spine bent to conform with the pattern, and the center of gravity placed appropriately), and some more difficult. Most of these exercises were based on natural movements that the horse uses when at liberty. By working the horse daily, the trainer developed the animal's muscular strength, agility, and obedience. Only after he had been so conditioned and trained was he ready for the "off-the-ground airs" just described.

As hand-to-hand mounted combat disappeared from the battlefield after the discovery of gunpowder, the practical need for such advanced movements died away. Horses were still used in warfare however, and needed to be maneuverable over rough country as well as under the frightening stress of fighting. They were also used for hunting and as riding mounts. So trainers continued to use the basic systems of training developed by the old masters to make the horse strong, willing, obedient, and agile. Thus, because he obeyed the rider instinctively, the hunter or the jumper could be taught to face obstacles which, if left to himself, he would avoid from fear. The horseman with educated hands and the necessary tact could have the pleasure of riding and exhibiting a horse that was not only more comfortable to ride than was the untrained horse but performed movements beyond the ability of the average animal. He could thus exhibit his own skill and the training of the horse and compete in classes designed to test this skill.

This system of training is known as "dressage" training, the word being taken from the French verb *dresser*, meaning "to train." It is equivalent to the special exercises practised by all athletes, from ballet dancers to boxers, and for the same purpose. It is now divided into three stages: basic dressage, necessary for the training of all riding horses; intermediate dressage for good horsemen who want a highly trained, flexible animal or who intend to compete or exhibit; and advanced dressage, which includes off-the-ground movements. (There is still one profession which demands knowledge of intermediate dressage, for on its proper execution depends the life of the rider. This is the type of bull fighting in which the bullfighter is mounted, as widely practised in Portugal and sometimes in Spain and Mexico.)

The basic principle of English training is that the rider must be in constant communication with his mount. He must be able to influence his horse instantly so that the latter will instantly vary his speed, his gait, and his direction, even to the exact placing of an individual foot, according to the command received through the rider's "aids." The latter are comprised of the hands, which work through the reins to the mouth, the legs, back and distribution of the weight. It follows that the English-trained horse must never be ridden on a completely slack rein. If this happens the rider is no longer in direct communication with his mount; he cannot obtain immediate response for he must first set up this line of communication. The first thing the young horse must learn after he has received his early training described in the previous chapter is to "accept" the bit: to like the feeling of slight pressure on his bars or in the corners of his lips and to wait for and depend on this as well as on receiving commands from the other aids before executing any new change of movement, gait, or direction. He must never fear the bit as a form of punishment for not obeying quickly but must be willing to go forward and increase his speed and extension against the pressure of it.

This is completely contrary to the way the Western horse is schooled. For him, pressure on the bit means only one thing: stop. He has learned that unless he obeys this signal of the bit to stop, grave discomfort will result. He is never asked to accept the bit in the way the English-trained horse accepts it. Therefore it is extremely unwise to take a horse of any breeding that has been trained for Western riding and expect him to adapt to English training. Nor should one expect a dressage horse ever to make a good cutting horse or cow horse. The basic training of each is too diverse. However, because his breeding and background give him the necessary physical and temperamental characteristics, the American Quarter Horse can be trained for work on the ranch and for successful competition in Western classes *or* he can be trained as a hunter, jumper, race horse, or dressage horse.

The Western-trained horse, like the English-trained horse, is first taught to give the rider a comfortable ride. He must learn to start, stop, and turn quietly, obediently, and in a natural manner.

WESTERN
TRAINING

The rider may work him in a corral, as shown here on the Cauble Ranch, or . . .

out in the wide range country, as Susan Boland is doing. Much of the early training is done in a bosal or a hackamore. These do not have bits, the only pressure being on the nasal bones. For aids the rider uses his weight in the direction of the movement and slightly back for decreasing the gaits and stopping. For turning he teaches the horse to respond to a slight pressure.

The next thing he must learn is to turn away from a light pressure of the rein on the neck. The rider puts his weight slightly toward the inside curve of the turn and still over the center of the horse. This is practised at all gaits until at the lope, as shown here, the horse will circle in either direction, bending his body naturally in the curve of the circle. Following this, the horse is taught to go from a circle in one direction to a circle in the other. The training starts at the trot. When the horse has learned what is expected of him, he is required to execute

Courtesy of A. S. Barnes.

it at the canter. This requires a "flying" change of lead, a difficult movement but one which constant practice makes perfect. The rider uses a change of weight and a shift of the active rein from one to the other to demand this change. Remember that this training is usually started in a hackamore.

More advanced training is taught when the horse is required to come to a sudden stop. This work is usually started in a corral where the horse can be headed for the fence at a lope. Since the fence is a natural barrier that the horse respects, it is not hard to get across to him that when the rider sits down and back and lifts his hand holding the rein, the horse is expected to throw his weight back onto his haunches, plant his hind legs, and slide to a stop.

Here ELM'S NYLON LADY owned by W. W. Underwood comes to an excellent sliding stop. Notice that the horse is executing the movement smoothly, with no resistance, showing good training and good riding on the part of Paul Babington, who is in the saddle.

Courtesy of W. W. Underwood. Photo by "The Eastern Quarter Horse."

The important thing at this stage of training is to carry the horse along slowly and not demand too much. The horse shown here is stiff in the poll and the mouth is slightly open; obviously too much is being expected of him.

From "At the Horse Show," by Margaret Cabell Self. Courtesy of A. S. Barnes.

From "At the Horse Show" by Margaret Cabell Self. Courtesy of A. S. Barnes.

The turn on the haunches which will later develop into a spin is performed with the weight of both rider and horse thrown back. A slight tension on the outside rein (the one opposite the direction of the turn) against the neck both indicates how he is to turn and prevents him from moving forward. This movement, which is executed from a halt and is demanded in both directions, is not only required in reining horse and cowhorse patterns but is used constantly by the cutting horse in adjusting his movements to those of the animal being worked. In the movement as taught in Western training the horse keeps both hind feet planted while he raises his forefeet off the ground and pivots in a half circle. He is so taught because speed in the finished movement is essential. As will be shown later in this chapter, the English-trained horse is also taught to turn on his hindquarters, but since speed is not essential the movement is slightly different.

Another figure required in the reining pattern is the rollback pictured in the accompanying three photographs. It is developed from the turn or spin on the hindquarters. The horse proceeds at a good speed past a marker, then sits down and rolls back over his hocks as in a sliding stop, but turns as he does so, so that he ends up going in the reverse direction. The whole figure must be executed with a continuous, fluid motion. There can be no actual halt for even a fraction of a second. Needless to say it is an extremely difficult movement to do well.

Here EASTER CODY executes the rollback in almost perfect form. Having just passed the marker, she slides and turns.

Courtesy of C. T. Fuller.

Forward motion has stopped, but she is pivoting on her hind legs, both of which are fixed.

The turn of 360 degrees practically completed she is already taking off again.

The conditions under which horses work and show are not always perfect, especially as to footing, as shown by Billy Allen, All-Around Champion, working out on a wet day.

THE CUTTING HORSE

Not every horse has it in him to make a good Cutting Horse. He must be born with the instinct to follow the calf or steer of his own accord. Most trainers try their young stock out and, if at the end of a few trials the colt shows no aptitude, his training as a Cutting Horse comes to an end and he is prepared for some other career. The following five pictures were taken by the author at the Cauble Ranch and show Mr. Cauble working with a promising three-year-old, son of Cutter Bill.

The lesson is given in one of the small, high-sided corrals, about 30 feet in width and 40 or 50 feet in length. The calf is worked back and forth across the short side of the corral. Mr. Cauble starts the calf by turning him away from one wall while the turn-back man places himself so that the animal does not run along the wall but cuts back across the corral.

Of his own accord (shown by the dangling reins) the young horse turns with the calf and runs parallel to it.

As the calf reaches the fence he digs in his forelegs and stops. The horse puts on the brakes also, but notice that whereas the calf is on his forehand, the horse is bringing his hind legs under him.

The calf has turned; the horse is in the act of turning. Hind legs planted, he has swung his forehand completely around them in preparation for setting off in the new direction. The reins of the rider are still loose; he is giving no indication to the horse of what he should do and the latter is executing this most difficult balancing feat all on his own.

The role of the turn-back man is to keep the movements of the calf confined to a small area of the corral, thus forcing the cutting horse to maneuver his body as handily as possible. The turn-back man anticipates the direction of the action and tries to so place himself that the calf turns back toward the horse in training rather than away from him.

[63]

Having learned to follow the movements of the steer or calf in the small corral, the cutting horse must now learn to work with other animals in the ring. Here another of the progeny of Cutter Bill, PRINCESS CUTTER, 370,778 shows her agility at preventing the steer from going back to the herd.

Here and on the next page, CUTTER'S FIRST, P-137,220, a World Champion Cutting Horse, son of Cutter Bill, shows, at the age of four, some of the remarkable positions a cutting horse gets into when doing his job.

Working in the large indoor arena, another three-year-old, CUTTER'S BEAUTY, demonstrates the balance of the cutting horse. Examine the positions of the horse's legs, and you can see how in just a split second she must have stopped and changed direction.

Courage and determination are also needed in the make-up of a good cutting horse, for he must not flinch at times such as this where the steer shows every indication of being about to charge the horse and rider; here, HARDY'S JESSIE, ridden by Bob Anthony.

[65]

THE ROPING HORSE

It is the job of the Roping Horse to put himself into and stay in such a position in relation to the calf that the rider can rope him. Thus he, like the Cutting Horse, must learn to follow the movements of the animal of his own accord. He must learn one other thing. As soon as the rope is thrown and has fallen over the head of the calf, the horse at once must come to a sudden stop. The rope is fastened to the horn of the saddle. It is up to the roping horse to keep it tight while the rider dismounts, runs forward, and ties the legs of the animal.

In this picture the roper may have trouble: his extra rope is coming loose and one rein seems to be caught over the poll of the horse. None of this makes any difference; he is on his way, piggin' string in his mouth, to tie up the calf, though the calf is still in the act of falling and the horse is still sliding to a stop.

Courtesy of the AQHA. Photo by H. D. Dolcater.

To the real lover of horses, the winnings in the show ring are secondary to the personalities of the horses themselves. C. T. Fuller, who bred the sister Champion Mares shown here with trainer Bob Anthony, says that they are not only working horses but friends and companions as well. They are EASTER CODY and SAPPHO CODY, P-117,421, daughters of Joe Cody out of Hapgood's Sal.

Courtesy of Willow Brook Farms.

To understand how the English-trained horse is taught and how he is ridden, one should know how the rider uses his aids and how the horse responds to their use. Briefly, the horse is taught to move away from the pressure of either or both legs, to move in the direction of tension applied to the rein, to respond to a use of the back to bring his hind legs under him, and to carry his body toward the way the rider throws his weight. The rider does not always use his aids exactly the same way. Furthermore, he balances one against the other. Thus,

ENGLISH TRAINING

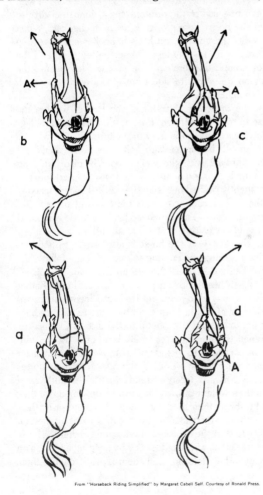

The chart will give the reader an idea of the various ways the rider uses his reins. These are termed "rein effects." Arrows marked *A* show the direction of tension on the rein. Arrows not marked with an *A* show the direction of the movement of the horse's body. Figure *a* shows direct rein of opposition. Tension is to the rear as well as to the side; horse slows his gait and turns to the left, hind legs following track of forelegs.

Fig. *b* is the leading rein. With no tension to rear, horse turns without slowing gait.

Fig. *c* is indirect rein of opposition. Tension is against neck but also to the rear. Horse turns to the right but brings his weight back and swings slightly on his haunches.

Fig. *d*. The indirect rein behind the withers is seldom used except in demanding the shoulder-in. It is a very strong rein effect, the tension being toward the horse's hip, and calls for a strong bending of the loin with the weight to the rear.

From "Horseback Riding Simplified" by Margaret Cabell Self. Courtesy of Ronald Press.

if the horse overreacts when a movement is demanded with one aid, the rider uses an opposing aid to counteract this. As an example, in executing one step of the pivot around the forehand, should the horse step too far or too fast in response to the use of the leg, the rider will oppose and control this movement by using his diagonally opposite rein.

When the rider wants the horse to curve his body (in making a circle or in executing the shoulder-in) he uses his leg against the girth on the inside of the curve with an assisting use of the opposite leg behind the girth to keep the horse from swinging his haunches out. When he wants the horse to push his haunches out or to step sideways with his haunches, as in the leg yield and the pivot around the forehand, he uses the leg behind the girth on the opposite side from the direction in which the haunches are to move.

In the first year of training, the trainer teaches the horse to travel on straight lines at all gaits, the hind legs following exactly in the track of the forelegs, and to come to a smooth but immediate halt. The horse should remain standing with the weight equally distributed on the four legs, head with poll and jaw relaxed, muzzle only slightly pushed out from the vertical, ears pricked— on the bit and ready to move out instantly at any gait and in any direction. This cadenced halt might be compared to the soldier halting to stand at attention.

In this first year the horse is also taught to bend his body in turning and circling so that his spine follows the curve being described. No attempt is made to "place" the horse's head at this time or to "collect" him. Rather he is encouraged to move out freely, to accustom himself to the feel of a light tension on the rein, to balance himself naturally, and to respond to the aids.

When the horse moves freely but correctly, his education continues to include other movements which are indeed difficult. We must first understand that horses moving forward freely extend themselves and travel with their weight thrown forward. In slowing down they tend to bring their hind legs under them and bring their center of gravity back. The rider makes use of this natural ability to shift the center of gravity and teaches the horse to change it at will. He does this by keeping a tension on the reins (but does not pull them more strongly); then, with back and legs, he drives the horse forward against the bit. The effect is to cause the horse to bring his head to the vertical and shorten his longitudinal length by bringing the hindquarters under him. This is called "collecting" the horse. To understand the purpose behind

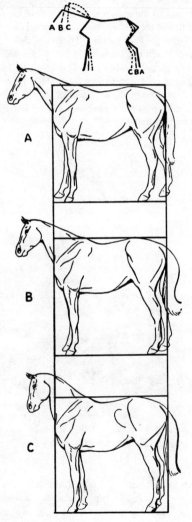

A   Horse naturally extended.

B   Slight collection, head more vertical, haunches slightly brought under normal position for horse in second stage of training.

C   Almost full collection, head more vertical, haunches further under. This is position for movements such as two-track, shoulder-in, etc.

From "Horsemastership" by Margaret Cabell Self. Courtesy of A. S. Barnes.

this one should visualize a springy switch bent to form a semicircle. Releasing the tension thus developed causes the switch to spring away from the holder's hands. Collection develops a like alertness on the part of the horse, preparing him to obey immediately any command given by the rider and so balancing him that he is able to obey that command immediately to the best of his ability.

The first exercises to promote collection are given while the horse is in motion. There are three phases of each gait which the horse must learn: the ordinary, the collected, and the extended. The thing to be remembered is that the cadence or beat made by the horse's hoofs is the same in all three phases but the horse travels faster or slower, as the case may be, by lengthening or shortening his stride.

HAPGOOD CHESTY, 71,843, owned and trained by Diana Dimon, is shown here executing the ordinary trot. The horse is crossing the ring on a diagonal. Notice how exactly his hind legs follow in the track of his forelegs and how straight the spine is.

Courtesy of Diana Dimon.

This is the collected trot. The horse's hindquarters could be a little more under him and his head a little more to the vertical, but a comparison with pictures of the extended trot shows how the horse has here shortened his stride and elevated it.

Courtesy of Diana Dimon.

In the extended trot, the horse is still strongly on the bit. In fact at the extended trot he should lower his head and lean on the bit for balance.

Courtesy of Diana Dimon.

Along with exercises in collection and extension, the horse is taught to move different parts of his body independently at the behest of the rider. The first of these is the pivot on the forehand. In this movement the horse pivots one step at a time around one foot, which may either be kept in place and turned on the ground or, better, lifted and replaced over the same spot.

Another example of the extended trot. This little horse, a second cross of Thoroughbred on Quarter Horse, was eighteen years old at the time this picture was taken. She had had very extensive dressage training, which shows in the exactly vertical profile, the strong use of the hindquarters, and extension that gives the appearance of almost floating.

From "Riding Step by Step" by Margaret Cabell Self. Courtesy of A. S. Barnes.

A second exercise, called "leg yielding," shown here from the rear, is one in which the horse, his spine kept straight and his body angled out from the wall, steps sideways, first with the forehand and then with the haunches. It is the first movement which the rider uses to put the horse on the bit and cause him to move one leg at a time, at the same time moving him along a specified line of direction.

From "Riding Step by Step" by Margaret Cabell Self. Courtesy of A. S. Barnes.

From "Riding Step by Step" by Margaret Cabell Self. Courtesy of A. S. Barnes.

In the pivot around the haunches, unlike the fast turn on the haunches of the Western-trained horse, the hind legs are not fixed but are lifted and replaced, the pivot leg coming down over the original print, the other describing a small circle around it. The horse takes one step at a time on the exact demand of the aids. In learning, he is required to stop as he makes the step but without bringing the feet together. This is the second step of the pivot around the haunches.

From "Riding Step by Step" by Margaret Cabell Self. Courtesy of A. S. Barnes.

The fourth step. Notice that he crosses the legs in front of the one which is stabilized, not behind.

The next to the last step and one of the most difficult. Later the horse will be trained to keep an even cadence in turning with no hesitation.

From "Riding Step by Step" by Margaret Cabell Self. Courtesy of A. S. Barnes.

The exercise of a pattern called "broken lines," in which the horse turns on the haunches as he changes direction, is introduced as soon as the horse understands the aids of the pivots. In this, the cadence remains the same when the horse is moving forward and when he turns. It is usually taught at the collected trot.

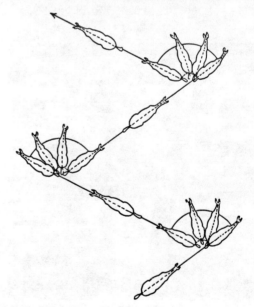

This is later developed into the turn on the haunches at the canter, also called the "pirouette." The horse, being on the rail at the canter, is made to put his weight on his inside hind leg and pivot around it as shown. This is the second step.

Courtesy of Diana Dimon.

The third step. The horse did the first steps well, but here he is not quite in balance and turns his head the wrong way to compensate, switching his tail to show his annoyance.

Courtesy of Diana Dimon.

[75]

We come now to one of the most beautiful of all the movements included in this phase of dressage training: the "traversal," or two-track, in which the horse leaves one wall and travels obliquely across to the diagonally opposite corner. He thus moves sideways and forward at the same time. His spine must be exactly parallel to the wall of the arena from which he began the movement, though the head may be bent at the poll slightly in the

The horse, in executing this movement, puts himself entirely into the hands of the rider. He is on the bit and is told by the rider when to take each step.

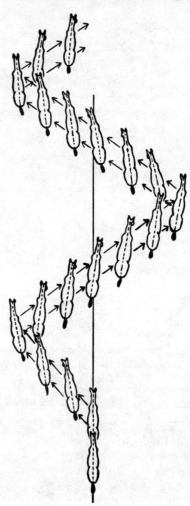

Here Hapgood Chesty (who has been shown in dressage competitions under the name of Hope Chest) executes the traversal or two-track at the trot, moving to the right.

Courtesy of Diana Dimon.

direction in which he is moving. As he moves he alternately crosses his feet by placing one front foot across and in front of the other and one back foot in front of and across the other back foot. He must never bring the feet across behind, and he must never let his forehand or his hindquarters get out of line. The movement is taught at all gaits and in both directions, the horse being asked to change from traveling along the wall to the two-track without shortening his stride or changing the cadence.

A further development of this movement is the counter change of hands on the two-track. The horse starts on the center line of the arena and, moving forward down it, displaces first to the left and then to the right, executing an equal number of steps on each side of the center line. This figure is especially effective when performed by four or more riders abreast moving in unison.

Three movements designed to improve the suppleness

of the horse's spine at the loin and to develop all his body muscles are the shoulder-in, the travers, and the renvers. All are very difficult. They are not based on natural movements of the horse but were developed during the fifteenth century by a famous riding master to King Louis XIII of France named Pluvenil. His book, in the form of questions (by the king) and answers (by Pluvenil), was published in 1660.

In the shoulder-in, the horse moves forward along the wall but with his forehand displaced toward the center and his body bent in an arch around the rider's inside leg, which is pushed against the girth. The hind feet are squarely on the track, the line from hip to hip of the horse being at right angles to the wall. The inside back foot follows in the trace of the outside front foot and the other two feet make separate tracks, so that the movement is one of three tracks.

Hapgood Chesty moves to the left on the shoulder-in. This is only a fair execution of the movement. His haunches should be more squarely on the track, and there should be more of a bend at the loin.

In the "haunches-in" or travers, the horse's forehand is kept on the track and his haunches pushed off the track toward the center. Whereas in the shoulder-in the horse was moving in the direction of the outside curve of his body, in this movement he is moving toward the *inside* curve, a far more difficult feat.

The renvers is a still more difficult movement. The horse's shoulders are square to the wall but they are off the track, the hindquarters being pushed toward the wall. Again the movement is toward the inside curve of the horse's body. The most important thing to remember in the execution of all these lateral flexion movements is that the spine must bend in a smooth circle from poll to tail. The neck must not bend sharply with the body being held straight.

There are many other even more advanced movements for which the horse can be trained. These include the flying change executed at every step; the piaffe, where the highly collected horse trots in place; and the passage, developed from the piaffe, which is an extended trot with great elevation as well in which the horse holds his diagonal legs raised for a perceptible instant. But these movement are only for the specialists and the horses that are especially talented.

Little has been said about jumping training. Here it is of the utmost importance that the horse not be rushed. He should be kept over low obstacles (not over eighteen inches or two feet) until he can negotiate them easily and without increasing or decreasing the gait. He should have practice over all sorts of unusual things: perhaps a bar with a coat hung over it or with a row of pails dangling. Many trainers use the cavaletti to start jumping training. This is a row of eight or more bars laid on the ground parallel with each other and about four feet apart. Eight feet ahead of the last is a low jump. The horse trots over the cavaletti and then canters over the obstacle. The effect is to steady the horse and put him in stride for the jump.

Many trainers also begin the jumping training on the longe without a rider. The main thing is to teach the horse to use his whole body, to be relaxed, and to judge his take-off correctly. It has been the author's experience that starting the training in a loosely fitting hackamore to avoid the possibility of inadvertently jerking the bit is best. The rider should not attempt to steady the horse at first but should let him make his own mistakes and correct them for himself. Later, when the horse is well trained, the rider must learn to keep a light contact with the bit so that the horse is always in communication. This is especially important in classes requiring many unexpected changes of directions, for it is often necessary to prepare the horse for the change while he is still in the air over the previous jump.

The next four pictures show Mrs. B. F. Allday using the longeing technique to train DYNAMITE RIKER, 367,724, a three-year-old filly, to jump. She starts by circling the filly quietly to one side of the low jump, the diagonal of the circle being in line with the bar. When the filly is going quietly and shows no fear, Mrs. Allday takes a step toward the obstacle, so that without changing the pattern the filly finds herself approaching it in such a manner that it is easier to jump it than to avoid it.

Photo by Winants Bros., Inc.

Green horses, unused to judging the height of a bar as they approach it, almost always overjump. This is because, owing to the way their eyes focus, they cannot see it clearly. If there had been a rider aboard, this very high jump might have caused him to come back on the horse's mouth and so sour her for jumping. Here is one of the many reasons why this method of schooling is good.

Photo by Winants Bros., Inc.

As it is, Dynamite is undisturbed and lands calmly.

Photo by Winants Bros., Inc.

With experience the young horse learns to judge his jumps correctly. Not until this stage is reached is he permitted to jump higher.

Photo by Winants Bros., Inc.

Part IV

Quarter Horse Shows

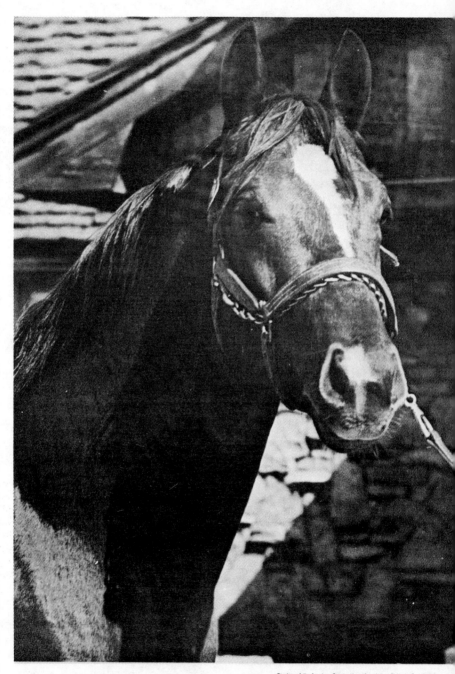

A characteristic and very beautiful American Quarter Horse head: note the delicate muzzle, the breadth between the eyes, the muscular jaw. It is that of El CHARRO ROCKET 424, 042, owned by O. M. and Lucille Starlin.

In the early days, as we have seen, Quarter Horses were valued for their racing abilities. Breeders introduced various bloodlines and selected those horses showing Quarter Horse speed and characteristics in order to provide animals to the colonists for their pleasure and sport. When this interest died there was still a large market for Quarter Horses as working animals on the ranch.

Unquestionably there is still this demand, as well as for the horse most suited to Youth Activities. This, however, does not explain the unprecedented increase in the registrations not only of Quarter Horses but of all types of horses in the United States. Today there are more horses bred, trained, and sold here than ever before—and this when it was predicted that the advent of the automobile meant the disappearance of the horse. The answer lies in the enthusiasm for showing. This, in turn, is the result of organizing shows on a nationwide basis and of awarding cash prizes and trophies which make the competition in shows worthwhile. The reason why the growth of registrations of the Quarter Horse has outstripped that of all other breeds of horses is due to the excellent job done by the department in the American Quarter Horse Association that is in charge of horse shows.

Before being eligible to be recognized as an "Approved" show, an application for approval must be made to AQHA. Such an application, made sixty days before the date of the show, will include such things as names and qualifications of the judges, number and description of classes, total number of entries, and total prizes anticipated. (If this show has been held previously, these are taken from the records of the previous year.)

If the AQHA accepts the application, the show is then recognized as an Approved Show, it is eligible to receive the trophies donated by the Association to all Approved Shows according to their classification, and the winners in the classes receive points toward their Championship and Registers of Merit classifications.

An AQHA-Approved Horse Show is open only to horses registered in one or the other of their registers (Permanent, Tentative, NQHA, Appendix, or New Appendix). It must be open to all Quarter Horse owners in good standing, and all show fees must be the same to all exhibitors. Rules for judging, class routines, and so forth as laid out in the AQHA rule book must be adhered to. At the show, each stall must exhibit the pedigree of the horse using it on a chart not less than ten by twelve inches.

Generally speaking, an exhibitor may enter in only one class of any category in any one show, but he may be entered in any number of classes of different categories for which he qualifies. Thus a cutting horse may show in only one cutting class, but he may also show in Reining, Working Cowhorse, Barrel Racing, and so on. This is one of the ways in which the AQHA rules for approved shows differs from those of the American Horse Shows Association, where no such limitation is imposed. The AQHA rule is a wise one, limiting as it does the number of exhibitors in any one class. Under other rules, classes are becoming so crowded that there may be over seventy entries in one class and the show may run several hours overtime. It must be remembered, however, that with the variety of classes offered in AQHA shows, the exhibitor has a chance to show his horse several times and so make the trip worthwhile. In the AHSA programs where a jumper is suitable only to show in Jumper classes, a Hunter in Hunter Classes, etc., the rule of only one such class for each entry would mean that many exhibitors would not think it worth either the money or the time and trouble to attend.

The point system (now all full point) is based on the number of entries in the class as shown

Number of entries	Placings and number of points					
	1st	2nd	3rd	4th	5th	6th
5–9	1					
10–14	2	1				
15–19	3	2	1			
20–24	4	3	2	1		
25–29	5	4	3	2	1	
30 and over	6	5	4	3	2	1

Show classifications are as follows: Class A—those shows with 225 or more entries; Class B—150 to 224 entries; Class C—75 to 149 entries; and Class D—24 to 74 entries.

In sex divisions, the Grand Champion will receive one point more than any other horse over two years old in that division. The Reserve Champion will receive as many points as any other horse in that division.

Points won in performance contests or in racing will qualify a horse for the Register of Merit, the purpose of which is to establish a record of performance. There are two Registers of Merit: one for working events and one for racing. The point system and rules of the Register of Merit for racing are in Part VI; point systems and Registers of Merit for Youth Activity classes will be found in Part V. To qualify for a certificate of Register of Merit, a horse must have won 10 points in one category with at least 5 in one event in an Approved Performance Class at an Approved Show.

The title of AQHA Champion may be awarded to a stallion, mare, or gelding that has won 30 points or more in competition in Approved Shows, provided that such points have been won in two or more shows under two or more different judges; and at least 12 of the points have been won in halter classes, and of these 12 a minimum of 4 points in either A or B shows, and that at least 12 points have been won in performance classes. AQHA Champions receive certificates to show the awarding of the title.

To win the title of Supreme Champion and the trophy that goes with it, a horse must have been Grand Champion at two or more Class A shows under two or more different judges. The horse must have won 40 points or more in recognized halter and performance classes at Class A shows, as follows: 15 points in halter classes, 20 in performance classes, of which 8 must be earned in one or more of the following: Reining, Working Cowhorse, Western Pleasure, Western Riding, or Jumping; and with 8 to be won in one or more of the following: Calf Roping, Steer Roping, or Registered Cutting.

The AQHA also maintains an Honor Roll, to which the horse in each division that has won the most points in that division in any one year is nominated. In case of a tie in one division, both horses are nominated. After

Halter Classes

the decisions have been made, a brochure containing pictures of the honor roll winners of that year is published. A list of these as well as a list of all newly titled Champions is also included in the booklet of the annual convention.

A halter class is judged on condition, including "bloom;" soundness and way of going at the walk and jog trot when shown on the line; and conformation (general build and proportions as well as muscular development).

Registration requirements to show are as follows: Stallions and mares two years old and younger must be listed in the Appendix or New Appendix. Weanlings and yearlings must be eligible for listing in the New Appendix stud book of the AQHA. Stallions and mares three years old and older must have a registration number in the official stud book. Geldings may show at any age on an Appendix or New Appendix number.

In the halter class, horses are led into the ring at a walk and then lined up as specified by the steward or the judge. At the latter's request, each horse is then led out of the line-up and shown at a walk and the jog trot in front of the judge along a center line of the arena: usually trotting from both directions, slowing or stopping, and turning at the end of the line as instructed. When dismissed by the judge the horse then returns to his position in the line-up.

These two Quarter Horse mares have a double registration, being registered in the Palomino book also. They are shown here winning a class for Palomino mares of any breeding.

Courtesy of A. S. Ba

After all entries have been shown, the judge passes along the row of lined-up contestants and gives each a thorough scrutiny from all sides. Unless he wishes to see certain ones again jogged on the line, he may now designate those he desires to place and have them moved out from the first line-up to a new line-up.

Courtesy of A. S. Barnes.

Some Outstanding Halter Champions

CACTUS KATHY, 94,779, was Grand Champion Mare at the 1968 National Western Quarter Horse Show at Denver, Colorado. This mare, owned by Kathryn Berwick, has won many trophies and ribbons for her young trainer and rider.

Courtesy of Lee Berwick. Photo by Darol Dickinson.

JUDY NUGGET BEE, 187,031, is another Grand Champion Mare. Foaled in 1961, she was named Grand Champion at the 1967 Pacific National Quarter Horse Show at the San Francisco Cow Palace, a show with over a thousand entries.

Courtesy of Sandee Proctor and Mrs. A. J. Ligthart.

LADY EVELYN'S PRIDE, 21,481, is an example of a mare that "came back." Thelma Chrisler bought her when she was fourteen years old from a farm family where she had been turned out for seven or eight years, being used only occasionally for trail riding. Although Mrs. Crisler had had little show experience, she conditioned the mare and started showing her in Long Island in Halter Western Pleasure, Reining, and Stock Saddle Seat classes. After the first few shows she placed or won consistently in every class, ending by being named Reserve Champion in Judged Events, Ladies' Division, for Long Island.

Courtesy of Thelma Chrisler.

TABBY DEXTERITY, 251,519, shown here by Karen Coffee, has over 100 points in halter classes. She is by Wimpy the Cat by Wimpy II out of Piu Dexterity by Poco Piu Mosso.

Courtesy of Coffee Bar Ranch. Photo by Ruby Loos.

RED MOORE MAC, 158,408, is a beautiful example of a Grand Champion Gelding. Note the square proportions of the body, the well-set-on legs, the beautiful bloom on the coat, and the general picture of strength and stamina.

Courtesy of Lee Berwick. Photo by Roger Wilson.

Two prize-winning fillies by TOP MAJESTY, 298,986. Dam of the near filly is My Pistol Pearl, P-38,512, and that of the filly on the far side Pearl King, P-114,703.

Courtesy of Mrs. Merle Mahoney.

A famous Champion and sire of Champions is shown here under tack, WIMPY LEO, P-125,571. His rider is Miss Patricia Faitz, who assisted with his show career and was the rider in the completion of his AQHA Championship. He is the sire of 1966 Reserve World Champion Mister Wimpy Leo and has been shown throughout the United States.

Courtesy of C. W. Minges. Photo by Tom Ester.

Our Canadian neighbors are fully as interested in the breeding, working, and showing of the Quarter Horse as are we. In their Association only horses with AQHA registrations are recognized. As in this country, their Association has been the fastest growing of any breeding associations, and there are more Quarter Horses registered than horses of any other breed. Here are three Quarter Horses belonging to the Bohomolec Ranch, Coleman, Alberta. They took all three Grand Championships at the Northwest International Horse Show in 1966.

Courtesy of A. and C. Bohomolec.

The horse on the left is TEREK, 204,733, by KING FIVE, P-72,607, out of ROSIE HANCOCK II, 100,618. On his sire's side Terek traces back to Wimpy, P-1, through Silver Wimpy, P-3507. Terek was show Grand Champion Gelding.

The mare in the center, being held by Mrs. Bohomolec, is AMBER GINN, 311,285. She is by Beaverdam Beaver, P-79,466, out of Ginger Five, P-79,469. She was foaled in 1964 so was only a two-year-old when she won this Grand Championship Mare award.

The horse on the right is KING FIVE, P-72,607, sire of Terek and named Grand Champion Stallion in this show.

Performance Classes

The purpose of this contest is to test the ability and manners of the horse from the viewpoint of his usefulness on the trail, across the fields, and in his everyday routine of chores around the ranch. Ordinary working equipment is required, no extra points being given for fancy equipment. Severe bits, tiedowns, etc., which would indicate a difficult animal are penalized. Only standard horseshoes are permitted. Only one hand may be used, the hand to be around the reins, but one finger between the reins is permitted; spurs or romal not to be used in front of the cinch.

Horses assemble outside of the ring before the class and enter one at a time to perform the pattern shown. They are judged on riding qualities at the walk, trot, lope, and change of leads; on the execution of the different movements; on manners, disposition, and obedience. Conformation does not count. A horse may be entered in only one Western Riding Class in each show.

The same specifications as to equipment, apparel, and method of holding reins apply as in the class for Western

WESTERN
RIDING HORSE

WESTERN
PLEASURE HORSE

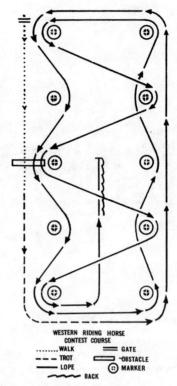

WESTERN RIDING HORSE
CONTEST COURSE

.... WALK   ═══ GATE
– – – TROT   ▭ OBSTACLE
——— LOPE   ⊕ MARKER
～～ BACK

riding horses. The rider carries the reins in one hand, which must be clear of the saddle while the horse is in motion. The horse is judged on smoothness of gait and tractability.

The horse shows along the rail at the walk, trot, and lope, reverses toward the center, may be asked to ride at all gaits in both directions, and must be asked to lope in both directions so that his ability to take the correct lead can be checked. At the discretion of the judge, conformation of the horse may count in the judging.

Generally horses work at all gaits in both directions. They must do so at the lope so that the judge may see that the horse uses the correct lead.

From "At the Horse Show" by Margaret Cabell Self. Courtesy of A. S. Barnes.

Having shown on the rail, the class is lined up by the judge so that he may have a look at them standing. At the discretion of the judge, conformation may also count in Western Pleasure Horse Classes.

From "At the Horse Show" by Margaret Cabell Self. Courtesy of A. S. Barnes.

RED BUDDY SORREL, P-116,052, an outstanding winner in Western Pleasure Horse classes, is shown here winning the American Royal Senior Pleasure Horse class, Quarter Horse Division, in 1967 for the third consecutive year. He has a total of 126 blue ribbons out of a total of about 185 showings, including the AHSA Men's Western Pleasure Horse at the Royal four consecutive years and the $500 Western Pleasure Horse Stake (open) at the Omaha Charity Show, and was Open Quarter Type Pleasure Champion in 1964, 1965, and 1966 of the Pony Express Horse Show Circuit. His rider and trainer, Robert A. Thomas, with no previous experience in preparing a horse for shows, found him tractable and intelligent.

Courtesy of Mr. Robert A. Thomas. Photo by William J. Stinson.

[95]

In addition to working at the three gaits along the rail in both directions, trail horses are asked to show their skill, willingness, and agility in negotiating various types of obstacles. There must be six of these, four of which are mandatory.

The mandatory obstacles are: opening, passing through, and closing gate; riding over at least four logs (or similar obstacle such as tires); riding over a wooden bridge; and sending horse freely into a horse trailer.

The optional obstacles are: negotiating water hazard (ditch or shallow pond); hobbling or ground-tying horse; carrying object from one part of arena to another; backing horse through L-shaped course; putting on and removing slicker; or dismounting and leading horse over obstacles not less than fourteen inches high or more than twenty-four inches high.

Since there is no set pattern established for the testing of trail horses, it is customary for the judge to meet with the riders before the class and explain to them exactly how he wants them to take the course.

The first obstacle is often a gate. SAGE MO, 215,401, ridden by Miss Brennie Grant in the Santa Barbara National Show, approaches quietly from the side and stands while the rider opens the gate . . .

Courtesy of A. S. Barn

goes through, and closes it again, all without letting go of the latch with her right hand.

Courtesy of A. S. Barnes.

Courtesy of Debby Dempsey. Photo by Jane Fallaw.

Another of the mandatory obstacles consists of a row of rails laid on the ground, over which the horse steps. This is SHADY DEUCE, 212,077, ridden by Debby Dempsey to win the blue in the class for riders fourteen to seventeen years old at the California State Fair. Shady Deuce, since sold to Carolyn Hipp of Sacramento, California, was All-Around Performance Horse at the Grand National Quarter Horse Show at the Cow Palace in 1966. That same year he was Reserve Champion Performance Gelding, Pacific Coast Quarter Horse Association, and Reserve Champion Western Pleasure Horse, Northern California Professional Horseman's Association Show.

[97]

Sometimes a row of tires further embellished by brush is substituted for the rails.

From "At the Horse Show" by Margaret Cabell Self. Courtesy of A. S. Barnes.

Since narrow bridges are commonplace in trail riding it is natural that Trail Class competitions require that the horse show he knows how to negotiate these intelligently and without excitement.

Courtesy of A. S. Barnes

Sometimes the judge calls for a figure eight at the lope or for two circles, one on the left lead and the other on the right, to be executed between the set obstacles. Such a test shows the handiness and obedience of the horse as well as his knowledge of leads. This is the sorrel gelding CASINO, 83,200, ridden by Cynthia Willis.

Rider Don Kilbourne on PANCHO, 20 demonstrates the test of backing quietly in a figure-L pattern.

Courtesy of A. S. Barnes

WORKING COWHORSE CONTESTS

The characteristics of a good working cowhorse as set up by the AQHA are as follows: The horse should have good manners; he should be shifty and smooth and have his feet under him at all times and when stopping, his hind feet should be well under him; the horse should have a soft mouth and should respond to a light rein, especially when turning; his head should be maintained in its natural position; and he should be able to work at reasonable speed and still be under control of rider.

Points to be penalized are: switching tail; exaggerated opening of mouth; hard or heavy mouth; nervous throwing of the head; lugging on bridle; halting or hesitation, especially when being run out, indicating overtraining and a disposition to anticipate being checked; losing the cow or leaving pattern unfinished because of a bad cow (penalty at discretion of judges).

Normal western attire, stock saddle, and ordinary grazing, snaffle, curb, half-breed, bar, or spade bit are permitted. No wire curbs, no curb strap narrower than one-half inch, and no nosebands or tiedowns may be used. The rider carries a rope or riata; spurs are optional.

Note that although Stock Horse contests are not among those listed by the AQHA, they are often part of a Western show program. All the foregoing specifica-

The pattern for working cowhorse and stock horse is ridden as follows: Beginning work either direction, (A) make first figure eight (B) and second figure eight (C). Begin run (D), come to a sliding stop (E), turn away from rail and begin second run (F). Then make another sliding stop (G), turn away from rail and make a short run (H), and a third sliding stop (I). Back up (J), make a quarter turn to the right (K), a half turn to the left (L), and a half turn to the right (M).

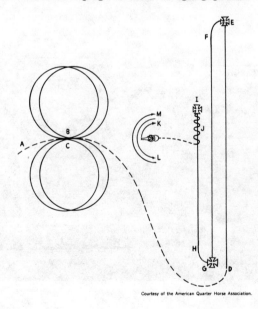

Courtesy of the American Quarter Horse Association.

tions apply to the judging of stock horses except the last, under points to be penalized. Inasmuch as the stock horse is not required to work cattle, this rule does not apply.

EASTER CODY, P-42,543, executes the counterclockwise circle of the figure eight. She was World Champion AQHA Honor Roll Reining Horse in 1965 and World Champion AQHA Honor Roll Working Cowhorse in 1966 and again in 1967. Note the calm precision of this movement: natural head set, body flexed slightly to conform with the pattern of the circle, weight well distributed.

T. Fuller.

SNIPPY REED, 64,980, ridden by Richard Downing, performs the circle to the left of the figure-eight pattern in a stock horse class in the Santa Barbara National. He too is well balanced, working willingly on a light rein.

From "At the Horse Show" by Margaret Cabell Self. Courtesy A. S. Barnes.

Not as well balanced as are the two horses shown above but the head carriage is good.

Courtesy of "The Quarter Horse Journal." Photo by Stacy Holmes.

This unusual picture of Easter Cody on the straightaway was taken at that split second when all four feet were off the ground.

Courtesy of C. T. Fuller.

HARLAN'S TYREE, 284,343, is shown here executing the sliding stop in a working cowhorse class. Notice the good head carriage, closed mouth, and good balance. This horse traces back to Wimpy, P-1. Winning his AQHA championship when thirty-three months old, trained and ridden by Dean Smith, he is a buckskin stallion, 15 hands, 1,200 pounds.

Courtesy of Carl Mills. Photo by Dalco Film Co.

Shady Deuce again, under the capable hands of Miss Dempsey, demonstrates the sliding stop as seen from behind.

Courtesy of Miss Debby Dempsey. Photo by Jane Fallaw.

The high, unnatural carriage of this horse's head in executing the sliding stop will mean a penalty on the judge's card.

From "At the Horse Show" by Margaret Cabell Self. Courtesy A. S. Barnes.

This is a bad stop altogether: head and neck are cramped, mouth is wide open, hindlegs bent and apart.

From "At the Horse Show" by Margaret Cabell Self. Courtesy of A. S. Barnes.

Backing as it should be done. The horse is relaxed and steps back freely and willingly, with no stiffness or resistance.

From "At the Horse Show" by Margaret Cabell Self. Courtesy of A. S. Barnes.

An example of how not to back a horse. Notice the tight rein, the open jaw, the ears pinned back, showing resistance, and the general stiffness of the body.

From "At the Horse Show" by Margaret Cabell Self. Courtesy of A. S. Barnes.

REINING CONTESTS

The purpose of a reining contest is to test the smoothness, calmness, willingness, obedience, and agility of the horse. The neatness, dispatch, and speed with which he performs the required pattern is also judged. Excessive jawing or head raising, lack of smoothness or breaking of gaits, stumbling, falling or wringing of tail, and attempts at disobedience such as backing sideways and knocking over markers are to be penalized. Also, any unnecessary aid on the part of the rider to get the horse to obey, such as petting, talking, or excessive use of spurs or quirt, will be penalized, as will changing reins from one hand to the other, carrying reins in two hands, or losing a stirrup.

As in Stock and Cow Horse classes, the class lines up outside and the judge explains what he wants. Any one of three reining patterns may be used. Classes may be limited to senior horses (five years or older), junior horses (under five years) ridden in bits, or juniors ridden in hackamores. The arena or plot should be about fifty by a hundred feet in size, and the patterns ridden at least twenty feet from any wall or fence.

Reining Pattern Number 1. The judge will indicate where to place the markers. Upright markers are mandatory at points marked X on pattern.

Ride pattern as follows: Run at full speed (A), stop, and back (B). Settle horse for ten seconds (C). Then ride small figure eight at slow canter (D-E) and ride large figure eight fast (F-G). Make left rollback over hocks (H) and right rollback over hocks (I). Stop (J), pivot left (K), and pivot right (L). Walk to judge and stop for inspection until dismissed (M).

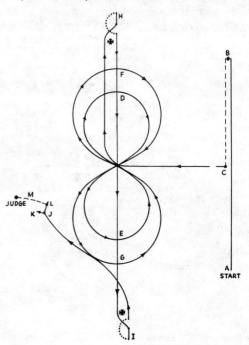

Courtesy of the American Quarter Horse Association.

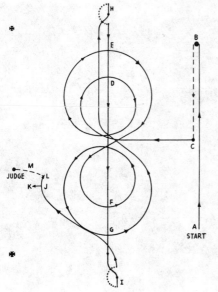

Reining Pattern Number 2.
The judge shall indicate the length of the pattern with markers on arena fence or wall, but kegs or other markers within the area will not be used.

Ride pattern as follows: Run at full speed (A), stop, and back (B). Settle horse for ten seconds (C). Ride two circles to the right (D-E) and two circles to the left (F-G). Proceed to the area beyond the point indicated by the marker on the arena wall or fence and do a left rollback over the hocks (H). Proceed to the area beyond the point indicated by the other marker and do a right rollback over the hocks (I). Stop (J), pivot left (K), and pivot right (L). Walk to judge and stop for inspection until dismissed (M).

Courtesy of the American Quarter Horse Association.

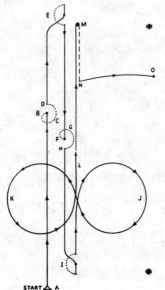

Reining Pattern Number 3
As in the previous pattern, the judge shall indicate the length of the pattern only with markers on the arena fence or wall.

Ride the pattern as follows: Run at full speed (A) and stop (B). Do a 360-degree spin (C), hesitate (D), and then proceed to area beyond the point indicated by the marker on the left arena wall or fence and do a rollback over the hocks (E). Stop (F), do a 360-degree spin (G), hesitate (H), and proceed to the area beyond the point indicated by the other marker on the arena wall or fence and do a right rollback over the hocks (I). Ride a figure eight (J-K). Run at full speed (L). Stop (M), back (N), walk to judge, and stop for inspection until dismissed (O).

Courtesy of the American Quarter Horse Association.

SKUNK FACE, 188,315, ridden
by Jimmy Flores, begins a
rollback in a reining class.
Skunk Face was Champion
Stallion Senior Working
Cowhorse in nation; top ten in
reining, High Point Reining
Horse for 1967, High Point
Working Cowhorse for 1967, and
Pacific Coast Quarter Horse
Association High Point
Performance Horse the same
year.

Courtesy of Mrs. James Flores. Photo by John H. Williamson, Sr.

HONDAS KING, 61,643 performs
the counterclockwise loop of
the figure eight.

Courtesy of "The Quarter Horse Journal." Photo by J. F. Abernathy Live Stock Photo Co.

A contestant in the Santa Barbara National Show breaks away fast after the spin in pattern number 3.

From "At the Horse Show" by Margaret Cabell Self. Courtesy of A. S. Barnes.

RED HOT PISTOL, Appendix Registered sorrel gelding, height 15:2, weight 1,250 pounds, is ridden here by Paul Horn of Springfield, Ohio. His sire is King's Pistol, 1967 World Champion Cutting Horse. Red Hot Pistol was Reserve High Point Senior Reining Horse of Ohio in 1967.

Courtesy of Bud and Carol Bodell. Photo by Ralph Crane.

KING REO, P-56,577, sired by King, P-234, received the following awards from the Empire State Quarter Horse Association: New York State Resident Senior Reining Horse, NYS Senior Working Cowhorse, and Eastern States Quarter Horse Association Pleasure Horse. He was also ESQHA Grand Champion Aged Halter Horse for the year 1965.

Courtesy of Harold D. Wood.

ROPING CONTESTS

Only the performance of the horse is judged in these roping contests. Time of the roper will not count against the horse. A time limit of two minutes for each contestant will be allowed. The roper may throw as many loops as are necessary, but if he has not roped the calf in two minutes he must retire from the ring. If he chooses to throw more than one loop he must carry a second rope and use this for the second loop. Should he carry one rope and miss the first loop he must retire, since without the second loop he cannot show how the horse will work trailing a rope.

The horse will be judged on the basis of 60 to 80, with 70 being considered average on the following: manners behind the barrier, scoring speed to calf, rating calf, the stop, working the rope, and manners while roper is returning to horse after tie is made. Breaking the barrier or any unnecessary whipping or jerking of reins or rope by the rider to make the horse perform better will be considered a fault and scored accordingly.

Calf Roping Contest

In the calf roping contest the rider, following the calf after it is released from the chute, ropes it around the head or neck.

Shown here is Jess Goodspeed, riding PISTOL'S HORNET, 247,103.

Dismounting immediately, he runs to the calf . . .

and ties its feet together. Meanwhile the horse has come to a sliding stop and is keeping tension on the rope.

The instant he has tied the calf securely, the rider holds up his hands to signify to the timekeeper and the judge that he is finished. The judge then comes up and inspects the knot.

**Steer Roping
Contests**

Steer roping has three classifications: Team Tying, Dally Team Roping, and Dally Steer Stopping. In the first two contests, two riders compete as a team with the horses being judged individually. The "header" heads the steer and ropes it; the "heeler" heels the steer and, after it is roped around the horns, head, or neck by the header, ropes it around one or both hind legs, jerks it down, and holds it while the rider of the header dismounts and ties it. In steer stopping, only one rider competes, and the steer is roped but not thrown and tied.

Wayne Garrett of Levant, Kansas, roping on KANSAS TWISTER, 300,029, at the Medicine Lodge, Kansas, Quarter Horse Show. Just released from the chute, the calf is racing, but the horse easily catches up and places himself a little to the side so that the rider can throw the rope.

Courtesy of the American Quarter Horse Association. Photo by Guy Kassal.

TENDER BOY, 54,822, was AQHA Honor Roll Roping Horse of 1961. He is ridden here by Floyd E. Orr, Jr., and shows the second stage of a roping contest, in which the rope is settling over the calf's head.

Courtesy of the American Quarter Horse Association.

Dave Clark on CASA GRANDE, 13,313, works fast. The rope has settled on the neck of the calf and the horse is in the act of sliding to a stop, but the rope is not yet tight and the calf is still at a run. The time to complete this contest was 13.9 seconds.

Sometimes it pays to dismount on the right. This is Stan Harter on the Champion Roping Horse SONITA Appendix Registered. His time was 10:5 seconds.

BARBY stands fast as the rider, piggin' string in teeth, runs forward to the calf that is just rolling over.

With raised hands Dean Oliver, seven times world calf-roping champion, signifies that his calf is ready for inspection.

Cutting Horse Contests are divided into two types of classes, Approved Cutting Horse Classes and Open Cutting Horse Classes (this class is run under the rules of the National Cutting Horse Association). An Approved Class is a class open to horses of any breed, age, and sex. A Restricted Class is one that is restricted to horses that fall within a certain category such as Seniors (over four years), Juniors (under five years), Registered Quarter Horses, or Palominos. Or the classification of the rider may be restricted, such as "For Junior Riders only" or "Ladies to Ride."

The American Quarter Horse Association lists its approved class as one in which only registered Quarter Horses may compete, with full points going to the winners. Such a class would not get full points in the National Cutting Horse Association records, whereas they would get full Quarter Horse points. However, all cutting horse classes have to perform and are penalized under the same set of rules.

Horses are worked in a series of "Go-Rounds," the number depending on the number of animals entered in the contest. Since they must enter the ring individually, it is best to limit the running of a Go-Round at any one performance to four horses. On the final Go-Round as many as six might compete, but more than that would be boring for the spectators and the cattle used would become too "conditioned." The National Cutting Horse Association recommends, for a show that is to run four days and has an entry of about thirty horses, that in the morning of the first day all contestants perform one Go-Round outside the show arena in a different area set aside for the purpose. The top sixteen are then set aside while the lower half compete again for a second Go-Round. Of course, careful point scores are kept of all riders. In the evening of the first day, four of the top sixteen compete for their score on their second Go-Round in the main arena before the public. Four more horses compete at the following performance, and so on. At the end of the fourth performance, all thirty horses will have scores for a first and a second Go-Round. Those with the highest total scores (number to be chosen being optional) then compete in the finals at the last performance on a third Go-Round.

In the contest, the cattle to be used are held in a herd at one end of the arena. (White-faced cattle in the year-

CUTTING
HORSE
CONTESTS

ling or two-year-old age are recommended, as they will provide plenty of opportunity to display the agility and skill of the horse.) Judges are mounted. Meanwhile, the contestant rides into the herd, selects the animal he wishes to work, and cuts it out, driving it a short distance away from the herd. The turn-back man, placed at an appropriate distance, turns the selected animal back and starts it toward the herd. The contestant then shows how the horse, working on his own, prevents the animal from returning to the heard. Generally two turn-back men are permitted, especially in cases of large or strangely shaped arenas or wild cattle.

The purpose of the contest is to select the horse that can cut out and control an animal with the least disturbance (to it and to the herd) and can show that he above all others is the best at working entirely on his own with no help from the rider.

Horses are penalized for the following: creating unnecessary disturbance; getting ahead of the animal and turning it back instead of letting the turn-back man do it; using the back arena wall as a turn-back wall; running into, scattering, laneing, or circling the herd against the arena fence while trying to head an animal; and turning the animal the wrong way with his tail toward it (he is penalized for this by being disqualified). A horse is penalized one point for every time the rider reins or cues him in any way or if the aids are used excessively.

Judge Byron Mathews riding WHIT'S LOLLIPOP shows how it should be done.

This was a close one. CUTTER'S FIRST, P-137,220, hasn't much room to maneuver but manages to stay on his feet. Sonny Perry is aboard.

Courtesy of the Cauble Ranch. Photo by Louise L. Serpa.

A son of Joe Cody, JOSÉ MELLIS, 80,972, with Ronald Stickley up. José showed as a novice cutting horse at the age of four. He was then retired and used as a lead pony at the tracks. Twelve years later he returned to his original career, and the following year he was shown fifteen times, winning or placing in twelve of these contests over some of the best cutting horses in the country.

Courtesy of Deane Fitz Hunter. Photo by M. H. Massey.

In the indoor arena at the
Houston Livestock Show, Jessie
Head rides AIR LOCK, 219,278,
in the cutting horse competition.
This sorrel stallion is by Parker's
Trouble out of Gold Question.

Courtesy of T. C. Livingston.

Matlock Rose, well-known
trainer, shows PEPPY SAN,
114,978, World Champion
Cutting Horse in 1967.

Courtesy of the Cauble Ranch. Photo by Dalco Film Co.

CUTTER JANE, 175,541, talented progeny of Cutter Bill, is shown here winning Gulf Coast Cutting Horse Maturity Class with John Carter up . . .

Courtesy of the Cauble Ranch. Photo by Jim Keeland.

Rodeo Events

Steer Wrestling is a rodeo rather than a horse show event. Two men and two horses and a steer that can and will run are used. The "hazer" keeps the steer going and blocks him from cutting away from the "wrestler." As soon as the steer is under control and on his way, the wrestler, throwing himself off his horse, grabs the steer as shown.

STEER
WRESTLING

This is Bill Alsbaugh making a successful grab. Notice that, whereas in roping the instant the horse feels the rider shift his weight for a flying dismount he slides to a stop, in wrestling he keeps going at a full gallop . . . to slow up only after he is sure that the rider has made a successful catch and is also putting on the brakes. The hazer also passes and then pulls in.

Courtesy of the American Quarter Horse Association. Photo by DeVere.

This is Bill Allen. Not only is he a Champion Steer Wrestler but All-Around Champion as well.

BARREL RACING

The next three contests test the speed and agility of the horse and are particularly suitable for rodeos and special events, as they provide the excitement which draws the spectators. Provided no error occurs, only speed counts.

Barrel Racing is the most popular.

SHAWNEE CASH, P-141,461, trained and ridden by Sharon Bowers, is winning first prize at the Antioch, California, fairgrounds. His sire is Super Cash by Spot Cash by Skipper W; his dam is Shawnee Sheik by Skipper W.

The course is of a cloverleaf pattern requiring three turns of 360 degrees. It is usually run to the right, the first turn being to the right and the two subsequent ones being to the left, but it may be run the other way. The contestant is allowed a running start.

Courtesy of Alia Thaden.

Mike Thaden had a mare named DIXIE. She was not registered, but she was an honest mare and at barrel racing, her specialty, she always brought home the ribbon. In the two short years he showed her she won forty trophies. It was then that they discovered that the mare was twenty years old!

Courtesy of Faith Dewel. Photo by Slore.

BUTCHER'S CODY, 213,621, trained and ridden by Faith Dewel, competes in the College Rodeo at Fort Collins, Colorado. This rider and mare competed successfully in 4-H Western riding when the latter was only two years and four months of age, placing third in a class of twenty-six.

Peggy Butler of Woodward, Oklahoma, riding TINY GLO, 187,677, in the Watonga Quarter Horse Show.

Courtesy of the American Quarter Horse Association. Photo by Guy Kassal.

POLE BENDING

As in Barrel Racing, the contestant starts behind the starting line at a run, time being taken as he passes it. The course is as shown. The poles are mounted in bases which sit on top of the ground and must be no more than fourteen inches in diameter. Knocking over a pole, or failing to follow the course spell disqualification. Either an electric timing device or two watches must be used. In case of a tie the winner must complete the second run within two seconds of the time of his first round.

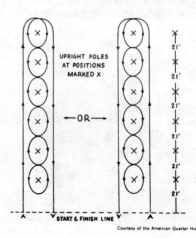

UPRIGHT POLES
AT POSITIONS
MARKED X

←OR→

21'

21'

21'

21'

21'

21'

START & FINISH LINE

Courtesy of the American Quarter Horse Association.

Courtesy of the American Quarter Horse Association. Photo by Guy Kassal.

Whip in mouth, Luann Corn makes the turn and starts back riding JAZZ KING.

Unlike Barrel Racing and Pole Bending, Flag Racing and the Rescue Race are not recognized as approved classes and so do not win points in AQHA-Registered Shows. They are very popular in other types of competi-

FLAG RACES

Courtesy of the American Quarter Horse Association. Photo by Guy Kassal.

tions, however, for they are fun for all: the horses, the riders, and the spectators.

The race is 130 yards. The rider must remove the flag from the can holding it. In so doing the can may be knocked over but not the barrel. In this form of the contest, which is run in heats, three or four riders to a heat, the barrels are placed in a straight line.

There is another form of Flag Race in which two barrels with flags in pockets are used. One barrel is on each

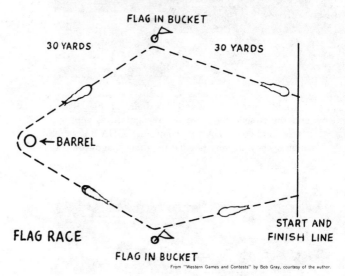

FLAG IN BUCKET

30 YARDS   30 YARDS

O ← BARREL

FLAG RACE

START AND
FINISH LINE

FLAG IN BUCKET

From "Western Games and Contests" by Bob Gray, courtesy of the author.

side of the arena and there are three flags, each of a different color. Riders ride individually. The rider is given one flag as he enters. He crosses the starting line and rides to the first flag, where he exchanges flags, continues past a barrel, keeping outside it, passes around the second flag, exchanging it for the one he carries, and races to the finish line. The trick is to make as much speed as possible between flags but to stop soon enough to avoid overshooting the next and to hesitate just long enough to make the exchange.

RESCUE RACE   All contestants line up at starting point. On signal, they race to the opposite end of the course (about 100 yards), pick up a partner behind a line, and then race back to the starting line. The partner must be astride horse at the finish.

WRIGHT'S LEO leaps forward under the guidance of Patti Mattox as Van Thompson scrambles aboard at the Fourth of July celebration at Derby, Kansas.

Classes for Quarter Horses Under English Tack

ENGLISH PLEASURE HORSE

The emphasis in English pleasure horse classes is on the ability of the horse to give a pleasant ride. Hence the judge looks for a horse with comfortable gaits, good manners, and what appears to be a willing disposition. Horses are usually shown in some type of Pelham bridle with a cavesson though full bridles and snaffles are permitted. The Saddle may be either the type used by saddle horse riders, with a cut-back tree, straight flaps, and a seat which throws the riders slightly back, or the modified forward seat type, with flaps cut forward and with a slight knee roll. The horse's mane and tail may be braided, but this is not required.

Horses enter at the walk. They then show the walk, trot, and canter in both directions. The rider should have light contact with the reins. He may be also asked to trot and canter without contact. In reversing, the horse turns toward the center. Note that while in Western classes the horse always turns toward the center, in English classes he does unless it is an equitation class (where the rider is being judged); in this case the rider pulls away from the wall and then turns back toward it. The walk should be smooth and animated but not choppy or shuffling. The horse should reach well forward with his back feet, and the print of his back feet should be well ahead of that of his front feet. The trot should be smooth, the action not high, but the horse should stride out. The canter should be an even three-beat gait. The head should be carried naturally, and the horse should appear relaxed and willing.

ENCHANTING, 197,502, owned and shown by Judith Feltman, is by War Chant, P-43,924, by Three Bars out of Miss Ark, 75,336, by Nevada King, P-13,320. She is a Grand Champion at Halter with 22 points and is well on her way to a championship rating in Performance, all her points being earned in English Pleasure. She is 15.3 hands and retains the good muscling of the Quarter Horse while showing the refinement of her Thoroughbred ancestry.

Courtesy of Mrs. W. T. Feltman.

JUMPERS AND HUNTERS

The general rules for the Quarter Horse Jumper are the same as those of the American Horse Shows Association, with two exceptions. Whereas in the latter a Jumper may enter as many Jumping Classes as he wishes in any one show, under the Quarter Horse rules he is limited to one such class. He may, however, also go into one working Hunter Class as well.

The other exception is that wings are permitted. In AHSA rules, wings are permitted only in Hunter Classes. Since these classes are comparatively new to the Quarter Horse owner, the AQHA has wisely kept its requirements simple. No stipulation is made that there be at least one change of direction in the course, and the minimum height is set at three feet.

In Jumper Classes a course of jumps is set up in the ring. A replica of the course is mounted at the entrance gate or near it so that contestants may memorize the order of the jumps. Sometimes this is also carried in the horse show catalog. There is generally a schooling area nearby with one or more obstacles over which entries may school just before entering the class. Many types of obstacles are permitted. The AQHA recommends that jumps be a minimum of three feet in height, set fifty feet apart, and that there be no fewer than four obstacles. Modern jump courses are usually designed to test not only the horse's ability to jump a given height over varied obstacles but also his flexibility and agility. Scoring is as follows:

Knockdown of obstacle, standard, or wing with any portion of horse, rider, or equipment . . . . . 4 faults.
First disobedience (anywhere on course) . . . 3 faults.
Second disobedience (anywhere on course) . . 6 faults.
Third disobedience (anywhere on course) Elimination.
Fall of horse and/or rider . . . . Elimination.
Jumping obstacle before it is reset or without waiting for signal to proceed . . . . Elimination.
Starting before starting signal; jumping obstacle before start, whether forming part of course or not; jumping obstacle out of order; off course
Elimination.
Failure to enter ring within one minute of being called . . . . Elimination.
Failure to cross the starting line within one minute after judge's signal to proceed . . . . . . Elimination.
Jumping any obstacle before crossing starting line unless said obstacle is designated as a practice jump
Elimination.
At a brush element, the touch of the brush only, without touching the framework or pole on top thereof, is not scored as a fault.

The AQHA rules do not specify what they term "disobedience." However, the following are usually recognized under this classification:
a   A refusal at a jump
b   A shy-out or avoidance of a jump
c   Taking an extra circle before taking the first obstacle.
d   Stepping backwards at any time after starting signal.

Mrs. Jon Riker is shown here holding ALFRED RIKER, 232,346, twice World's Champion Quarter Horse Jumper. He is wearing a Pelham bridle and a jumping saddle. Note that the flaps are cut forward of the pommel and have knee rolls. Since, in jumping, the rider shortens his stirrups to permit himself to rise out of the saddle and so take his weight off the horse's back as he jumps, the jumping saddle is so cut both to give the knee of the rider support and to prevent it coming in contact with the horse's shoulder.

Courtesy of Westenhook Farm, Inc.

EQUIPMENT

Flat saddles are used. The bridle may be either double, Pelham or plain snaffle. A curb chain may be used, but it must be at least one-half inch in width, cannot be twisted, and must meet the approval of the judge. Breastplate and martingales are optional.

Alfred Riker with Don Schmaling up takes a low chicken-coop-type obstacle with bar. He is now wearing a standing martingale, loosely adjusted so as not to interfere with the use of his head. Alfred Riker was Honor Roll Jumping Horse in 1966 and 1967. He earned 48 points in jumping and 4 as working hunter.

Courtesy of Westenhook Farm, Inc. Photo by Budd.

Another Riker horse called DENNIS RIKER, 371,014, with Mrs. Jon Riker up. The leaning panel simulates a chicken coop and encourages the horse to stand back at his jumps. Most horses jump more cleanly over an obstacle of this sort which looks solid than they do over obstacles such as post and rails which look as though they can be knocked down.

Courtesy of Westenhook Farm, Inc. Photo by "The Eastern Quarter Horse."

Dennis Riker over a brush jump made by setting palm fronds inside a crate. The bar on the far side encourages the horse to extend over the jump.

Courtesy of Westenhook Farm, Inc. Photo by "The Eastern Quarter Horse."

SASSY STEP, 274,753, with Don Schmaling up negotiates a post-and-rail jump made with striped rails. This type of jump is characteristic of jumper courses but would not be permitted in a hunter course, since in these natural rails must be used. Sassy Step is wearing a hunting snaffle with braided reins and no martingale, indicating that he has a light mouth and jumps willingly. His front legs are bandaged to prevent injury from inadvertent raps. The rider is giving the animal freedom of the head and neck but at the same time is keeping a light contact with the mouth.

Courtesy of Westenhook Farm, Inc. Photo by Frank Frasca.

CANDISUGAR RIKER, 312,481, with Sandy Vaughn up negotiates a triple bar in perfect form. Notice how well arched the back is and how the lowered and extended head completes the curve from poll to dock. Form does not count in jumping classes but would in hunter classes. On the other hand, we know that this is not a hunter class because of the type of jump.

Courtesy of Westenhook Farm, Inc. Photo by Tarrance.

Courtesy of Linda and Carol Savaglio. Photo by Kleppe.

STAR SPECIAL, Appendix Registered sorrel gelding, over a triple bar. He was foaled in 1958 and was a ten-year-old when this picture was taken. His sire was the Thoroughbred Kind Guy by another Thoroughbred, Kind Man. His dam was May Girl Uptegrove, 55160, by Mayflower. With his Thoroughbred bloodline he shows the finer type of conformation but appears to have the calm temperament of his Quarter Horse lineage. Star Special tied with Alfred Riker for the Honor Roll Jumper of 1967.

THE HUNTER

As in Jumper Classes, the Quarter Horse is allowed to show in only one Hunter Class in a show but may show in one Jumper Class as well. Equipment for both classes is the same. If the entries warrant, the class may be divided into two sections, Senior Working Hunter and Junior Working Hunter, based on the age of the horse. The same rules apply for both except that the minimum height for jumps in the junior division is three feet rather than three feet three inches. The use of wings is recommended. The course is left up to the judgment of the officials, but it is intended to test the horse as a hunter and not as a jumper, and light touches are not considered faults. For this reason it is recommended that the obstacles (there must be at least four) be placed at a minimum of fifty feet if possible, thus showing the horse's ability to go on and to test his wind, and the fences should simulate natural obstacles to be found in the hunting field.

In scoring, horses are judged on manners, the maintenance of an even hunting pace, a "hunting" style of jumping (in which the horse does not get too close to the obstacle and "pop" over it or take off too far away), way of moving, and soundness at the jog. In all classes judges line up horses on merit of performance before considering soundness. Horses may be required to show at a walk, trot and canter. All horses must be serviceably sound, and a horse showing lameness, broken wind, or impairment of vision is refused an award.

In judging faults light touches are not considered. Judges penalize unsafe jumping and bad form over fences whether touched or not. Faults for knockdowns, disobediences, and falls are the same as in the Jumping Class.

Equipment is the same as for jumpers. Note that here again the AQHA rule differs from that of the AHSA. In the latter, running martingales are permitted, standing martingales would cause a horse to be marked down.

BOB'S BAY KING, 484,907, sire Moon King, 75,224, by Major King, 14,005, dam Blue Grass, 14,025, by Little Joe Springer, was foaled in 1960. He was bred in Strasburg, Virginia, by Ronald C. Stickney, trained by Bob Allday, and owned and ridden by Mrs. Allday. He is shown here winning the working hunter class at the Virginia State Quarter Horse Show in September of 1968 at Herndon, Virginia. He was Honor Roll Working Hunter in 1967, with 13 points in Working Hunter Classes, 13 points in Jumper Classes and ½ point in Trail Horses Classes.

In between the jumps the hunter must gallop on but must not appear to be pulling or getting out of hand. Here Mrs. Allday brings Bob's Bay King along evenly. It was this type of form which won him first at the Chicago International.

Courtesy of Five Oaks Quarter Horse Farm. Photo by Winants Bros., Inc.

As the hunter approaches the next obstacle he pricks his ears and so regulates his stride that he is in stride for the take off. This alertness will bring Bob's Bay King extra points on the Judge's card.

Courtesy of Five Oaks Quarter Horse Farm. Photo by Winants Bros., Inc.

In the schooling field the jumps are solid. This is a panel of 6X10s set into a fence. Light brushes, such as the one here, would not count against the horse in a show, and the solidity of the jumps discourages him from hitting it hard. Mrs. Allday is just right for a jump of this height, not too high out of the saddle but with the weight over her stirrups. She is giving the horse plenty of rein so that his head can be used to balance and he can arch his neck and back, yet keeping in contact with him through the lightly stretched rein.

Courtesy of Five Oaks Quarter Horse Farm. Photo by Winants Bros., Inc.

Eleven-year-old Scarlett Allday rides three-year-old DARVELL RIKER, 368,557. The little black gelding is by Adam Riker, 247,163, by Royal Bar, 61,936, out of Hardie's Jane, 86,556, by King Clegg, 7443. This pair has not yet made its appearance in the ring, but Mrs. Allday has great hopes for their future.

Courtesy of Five Oaks Quarter Horse Farm. Photo by Winants Bros., Inc.

Part V

The Youth Activities Program

One of the most important and rewarding functions of the American Quarter Horse Association is the running of their Youth Activities Program. In these days of the automobile, most youngsters have no chance to care for farm animals. Even those who live on farms often learn to drive tractors and run mowers instead of working with horses. The 4-H Clubs maintain interest in breeding and fitting programs. Although young people like to compete in rodeos and in shows, they used to have to enter classes open to persons of all ages.

Anyone who has ever worked with horses knows that the opportunity to own, care for, train, ride, and show a horse is the best possible way to teach youngsters a skill and give them knowledge that will be useful to them all their lives. At the same time it gives them a healthy outlet for their energy and their inherent love for animals. Garford Wilkinson expressed the need for a youth program sponsored by the Association in an article in the *Quarter Horse Journal* early in 1959. A survey soon made of 4-H Club directors and leaders of Future Farmers of America group substantiated the original premise that where horses were available they were superseding the magnetic power of the jukebox and the hot rod.

The first program was a 4-H Club project for Quarter Horses initiated in Louisiana by the State Extension Service. Classes in judging, riding, and showing Quarter Horses in many types of performance competitions were provided for the young people of Louisiana. Then, in 1960, the AQHA established a Youth Activities Committee to supervise classes and shows limited to junior exhibitors and to perform related services.

The list of Youth Activities classes includes Barrel Racing, Breakaway Roping, Calf Roping, Cutting, Halter Classes, Jumping, Pole Bending, Reining, Showmanship, Stake Race, Trail Horse, Western Horsemanship, Western Pleasure, Western Riding, Working Cowhorse, Working Hunter.

APPROVED SHOWS
AND
CLASSES

Application to hold a Youth Activities show must be made in writing at least sixty days ahead and must include a list of all classes. Only a manager or a director with stated experience in adult or youth shows may make the application. A show must be open to all Quarter Horse owners eighteen years of age or under on January first of that year. Horses shown must be registered with the AQHA and must be the bona fide property of either the person showing or of his father, mother, brother, sister, grandparents, or guardian. Horses leased to one of these do not qualify.

A contestant may compete in only one class of a given category. The horse may only compete in only one class of a given category and not in another subdivision of that category under a different rider. Trophies are awarded by the AQHA for Halter classes (one each for Champion Mare, Champion Gelding); at least one class for each of these must be in the program, with a minimum of four entries per class.

To qualify for the All-Around Performance trophy, for the winner of the most points at an approved Youth Activities show, the contestant must have competed in at least three of the following approved classes; Showmanship at Halter, Cutting, Reining, Barrel Racing, Calf Roping, Working Cowhorse, Jumping, Working Hunter, and Western Pleasure, Breakaway Roping, Western

Kathryn Berwick with her Grand Champion Mare CACTUS KATHY, 194,779, receives the 1967 High Point Quarter Horse of Louisiana award.

Courtesy of Lee Berwick.

The Grand Champion Mare MORRIS QUEEN, 222,008, and her handler Lynn D. Smith. In addition to halter classes, this mare has been a winner in youth and pleasure classes.

Margaret D. Harris of Melbourne, Arkansas, on SNIPPER TOM, P-47,390, poses with her trophy after competing in the Buckaroo Pleasure Class in the Hillbilly Horse Show Association show at Ozark Acres Resort in Hardy, Arkansas.

Riding, Trail Class, Stake Racing, Pole Bending, and Western Horsemanship.

In general, the rules and performance patterns described in Part IV apply to the youth classes. However, except in competitions such as Barrel Racing, Pole Bending, and Stake Racing, all of which are timed events, consideration to the way the horse is handled and controlled must be given the performance of the horse.

SHOWMANSHIP AT HALTER

This class is limited to Youth Activities shows. Horses enter the ring counterclockwise at an alert walk, with exhibitor on the left. The horse is posed with feet squarely underneath animal. The exhibitor faces the horse while posing but should keep an eye on the judge,

Here Vernon Dickey, Jr., shows the fine halter mare MAGNOLIA NORMA, P-99372, at Valley Lodge, Texas. It was his third show. The blue ribbon which he won was well deserved, for he is following exactly the rules set up by the AQHA.

Courtesy of Mrs. Vernon Dickey. Photo by Agricultural Photo Service.

After watching the horses enter as a group and seeing them work individually, the conscientious judge passes along the line-up once more, examining each animal and each contestant with care. The condition, trimming, and grooming of the horse and the neatness of the exhibitor's appearance both count. The young lady shown here can hardly stand still with excitement under the judge's eye.

Courtesy of the AQHA. Photo by Guy Kassal.

Travers Brown, three and a half, showing MOE'S BARNEY, 308,854, is well aware of show decorum. Even though Judge H. L. Akin is looking at the horse of another entrant, he remains alert and does not crowd the exhibitor next to him. Perhaps he can't reach quite high enough to carry the lead in the right hand *close* to the halter as specified, but see how neatly the other end is coiled in his left hand!

remain alert, and continue to show the horse until all horses have been judged and placed or dismissed. Many a ribbon has been lost by young exhibitors who, as soon as the judge passed them, forgot that they were still exhibiting.

WESTERN HORSEMANSHIP

Western Horsemanship clothing should be neat, workmanlike, and clean. Chaps are used according to local conditions; tapaderos and spurs are optional. Any accepted type of saddle may be used, but it must be sized to the rider. A half-breed, spade, snaffle, or curb bit may be used. A curb chain, if used, must lie flat behind the horse's chin groove, when the reins are slack, so that fingers of the hand can be inserted without shifting the position of the bit. Hackamores, tiedowns, running martingales, and draw reins are prohibited; hobbles and reata optional. Silver equipment may be used but does not count more than good working equipment. Standardized horseshoes are preferred.

[141]

Competitors are judged on seat, hands, ability to control and show horse, and suitability of horse to rider.

Standards for correct performance are as follows: In mounting and dismounting the competitor should control the horse by taking up reins in the left hand and adjusting reins evenly with enough tension to feel the bit and hold the horse steady. Ends of the reins hang on near side while mounting. The rider should sit in the saddle with legs hanging straight and forward to the stirrups or knees slightly bent and weight directly over the balls of the feet. In either position the stirrup should be just short enough to allow heels to be lower than the toes. The body should always appear comfortable, relaxed, and flexible.

The left foot is placed in the stirrup (if necessary twist near stirrup with right hand). The competitor grasps saddle horn with right hand, springs up with right leg, keeping body close to the horse, and settles easily into the saddle. The right foot is slipped into the off stirrup and the rider assumes basic position. The horse should stand while being mounted until given the signal to move out. The end of split reins should be carried on the side of the reining hand. (A romal should be carried on the opposite side of the reining hand.) To dismount the above procedure is reversed and the rider steps down facing the horse's head.

Holly Fuller, here practicing for a Western horsemanship class on that fine mare, EASTER CODY, uses the seat with the slightly bent knee and the weight over the ball of the foot.

Upper arms should be in a straight line with the body, the one holding the reins bent at elbow, the free hand carried slightly above and in front of belt buckle. Only one hand should be used for reining, and hands are not to be changed. The hand should be around reins; fingers between reins are permitted when using split reins but not with romal. The reins are to be carried immediately above and as near to the saddle horn as possible.

Courtesy of C. T. Fuller.

Holly Fuller's position as seen from the side. The American Horse Shows Association flew Holly and Easter Cody to California to make the movie "The Principles of Stock Seat Equitation." The film is used extensively to present and define good form in Western riding.

In motion, the rider should sit to the jog and not post. At the lope he should be close to the saddle. All movements of the horse should be governed by the use of imperceptible aids. Exaggerated shifting of the rider's weight is not desirable.

In Western horsemanship classes, all horses enter the ring at a walk and are judged at a walk, jog, and lope. They are worked both ways of the ring and should always be on the correct lead. The reverse is executed away from the rail. The horse should be in perfect balance at all times, working entirely off his haunches; neck and head should be in direct line with the body; the mouth should be closed and the head at normal height.

After the horses have been worked in a group, they are lined up in the center of the ring. Then the judge may ask each horse to work individually. This includes many of the maneuvers normally required in a stock horse class, such as figure eights and square stops. Horses are required to back in a straight line in this class. Riders fourteen years and older are judged on form in mounting and dismounting; riders who have not reached their fourteenth birthday are not required to mount and dismount.

Some Young Performers in Action

Gary Day riding CHUCK'S CHUCKLE P116,646 opens the gate in a test in a Western Riding Class.

Courtesy of Peter W. Deleeuw, Jr. Photo by Bobbie.

Two Champions together. Fifteen year old Gary Weinberger, Res. Champion Open Western Rider for San Diego County Junior Horseman's Association Inc. on CHIQUITO JOE who has several Championships and Reserve Championships to his credit.

Courtesy of Dr. and Mrs. Harold Weinberger. Photo by Sam Stone.

Larry Matzke, riding CHUBBY PAPOOSE throws a pretty loop in a near perfect run at the Cotton Falls Quarter Horse Show in the Youth Break-Away Roping contest.

Photo by Guy Kassal

Art Dunlap on BRITE BLU BAR, 310,799, executes the sliding stop in an eleven-years-and-under reining class in Sante Fe.

Courtesy of Mrs. Noble Dunlap. Photo by Louise L. Serpa.

Before a young rider is ready to appear as an exhibitor, he and his horse must spend many hours in becoming a team. Here we see Holly Fuller on Easter Cody, working on cutting horse techniques.

Young Lewis Rex Cauble, son of Rex Cauble, well-known breeder of Cutting Horses and owner of Cutter Bill, also spends hours in the training ring. He is shown here on BLAZE FACE BILL, 227,899, one of Cutter Bill's many renowned sons.

Vernon Dickey, Jr., on RED COMET MAN, P-53,711, competes here in the barrel racing event at the Jones Bar J Ranch. Not only has Vernon had the pleasure of owning, caring for, training, and showing his horse and winning a wide variety of trophies in many different classes, he has had the opportunity of making firm friends in many states.

Courtesy of Mrs. Vernon Dickey. Photo by Agricultural Photo Service.

Sharon Joyce Larremore of the Circle L Cue Ranch in Holdenville, Oklahoma, competes in barrel racing on JOE REED L CUE, P-165,813, a horse she raised, broke, and trained herself. Sharon has won many prizes in Youth Activities classes: in 1965 she was State High School Champion Pole Bender and was selected Queen of several contests.

Courtesy of Circle L Cue Ranch. Photo by Spencer Studio.

[147]

Part VI

Racing

Courtesy of The Cauble Ranch.

HARD TWIST, P-5555, is now dead, but he was one of the greatest. In 1946 and 1947 he was World's Champion Racing Stallion. He was retired but returned to the track at the age of nine to be called the "Come-Back King" of racing when he co-held the title of World Champion Running Horse in 1951. He produced colts and fillies that proved his prepotence, and many of today's winners trace back to him.

Racing has come a long way since colonial days, but for many years there was no formal racing of Quarter Horses. In 1945, when the first records were kept, there were twenty-five recognized races. In 1967 there were 6,824, slightly fewer than in 1966, when there were 7,072.

From 1949 to 1968, a total of $44,221,430 was distributed in purses, with the annual distribution rising steadily from $146,398 in 1949 to $6,984,558 in 1967. On Labor Day of 1968 at New Mexico's Ruidoso Downs the largest purse in the history of racing was offered, a total of $602,000. The 400-yard All-American Quarter Horse Futurity is by far the richest race in the world, several times larger than the Kentucky Derby. In 1966 this same race had a purse of $430,000, with the winner, Go Dick Go, receiving $198,300, and in 1967 the purse was $486,593, with the winner, Laico Bird, taking $225,000.

The Los Alamitos (California) Racecourse added two 100-thousand-dollar purses in 1968, bringing the total prize money to be distributed in one year at this course to two million dollars. The two purses were for the Los Alamitos Derby for three-year-olds and the Kindergarten for two-year-olds. Other high-purse races in 1968 were the Rainbow Futurity at Ruidoso, with a purse of $79,178, and the Raton Futurity at Raton, New Mexico, with a purse of $93,000. The purse for the 1968 All-American Futurity totaled $602,000. The winning horse, Three Oh's, received 160,372 of the record purse.

With such large purses it is no wonder that the breeding and training of Quarter Horses for racing has become very big business indeed.

From 1949 to 1968, the Pari-Mutuel handled $694,867,503 on races for Quarter Horses, an increase from $1,807,418 in 1947 to $78,328,686 in 1968. These figures complete the picture of the money involved in this business of Quarter Horse racing.

EL CHARRO ROCKET, 424,042, is an example of what today's running horse looks like. He is rated AAA, having won his rating as a two-year-old. He was foaled in 1964 and started seventeen times in 1966, placing ten times with three wins, including the Jefferson Quarter Horse Futurity, where he won $1,674.75.

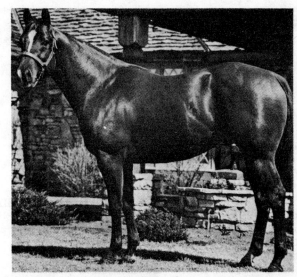

Courtesy of the AQHA. Photo by Guy Kassal.

The 1963 All-American Futurity at New Mexico's Ruidoso Downs. The purse that year was $285,000, only a fraction of what it was to become, but still the largest in the world, dollar for yard of distance.

Courtesy of the AQHA.

The finish of the All-American Futurity in 1968. First money went to THREE OH'S, who looks as though he were winning in the traditional fashion of sticking his nose out!

Some horses have consistent bad luck, such a one is M. T. POCKETS, P-17,922, shown here leading the field. He was bred by the Excelsior Ranch Company and carried on a career at stud at the same time that he was racing. He crossed the finish line ahead of many AAA horses, including HARD TWIST, yet for one reason or another was never rated higher than AA.

Although some fields are stretched out, as in this picture, showing ADAM RIKER ahead by several lengths, the majority of Quarter Horse racing finishes look like the one in the bottom picture, with six of the ten almost abreast and all ten running keenly. If this were a hunting picture and these fox hounds, the caption could readily be, "Hounds could have been covered by a blanket!"

[153]

This unusual racing picture shows both the "closed" and the "stretched" phases of the gallop. AIR CAPITOL, with all four feet off the ground, appears to be well ahead, and even the closest scrutiny cannot decipher what has become of the fourth leg of the horse behind!

Courtesy of the AQHA. Photo by Guy Kassal.

Index of Horses Pictured

The Author

Born in the hunt country of Virginia, Margaret Cabell Self says that she learned to ride before she could walk. After their marriage, the Selfs settled in Connecticut and Mrs. Self started each of her four children riding at the age of two. In 1929 she opened the Silver-mine School of Horsemanship and began to instruct professionally. Now the Selfs make their home on Block Island, off the coast of Rhode Island, and spend their winters in Mexico, where Mrs. Self is advisor-consultant of the Escuela Ecusetre of San Miguel de Allende, a Mexican riding school.

Famed as an authority on all aspects of horses and horsemanship, she is the author of nearly forty books, including HORSEMAN'S ENCYCLOPEDIA; HORSES: THEIR SELECTION, CARE AND HANDLING; THE COMPLETE BOOK OF HORSES AND PONIES; and THE MORGAN HORSE IN PICTURES.

A PERSONAL WORD FROM MELVIN POWERS
PUBLISHER, WILSHIRE BOOK COMPANY

Dear Friend:

My goal is to publish interesting, informative, and inspirational books. You can help me accomplish this by answering the following questions, either by phone or by mail. Or, if convenient for you, I would welcome the opportunity to visit with you in my office and hear your comments in person.

Did you enjoy reading this book? Why?

Would you enjoy reading another similar book?

What idea in the book impressed you the most?

If applicable to your situation, have you incorporated this idea in your daily life?

Is there a chapter that could serve as a theme for an entire book? Please explain.

If you have an idea for a book, I would welcome discussing it with you. If you already have one in progress, write or call me concerning possible publication. I can be reached at (213) 875-1711 or (818) 983-1105.

Sincerely yours,

MELVIN POWERS

12015 Sherman Road
North Hollywood, California 91605

MELVIN POWERS SELF-IMPROVEMENT LIBRARY

ASTROLOGY

_____ ASTROLOGY: HOW TO CHART YOUR HOROSCOPE Max Heindel 5.00
_____ ASTROLOGY AND SEXUAL ANALYSIS Morris C. Goodman 5.00
_____ ASTROLOGY MADE EASY Astarte 3.00
_____ ASTROLOGY MADE PRACTICAL Alexandra Kayhle 3.00
_____ ASTROLOGY, ROMANCE, YOU AND THE STARS Anthony Norvell 5.00
_____ MY WORLD OF ASTROLOGY Sydney Omarr 7.00
_____ THOUGHT DIAL Sydney Omarr 4.00
_____ WHAT THE STARS REVEAL ABOUT THE MEN IN YOUR LIFE Thelma White 3.00

BRIDGE

_____ BRIDGE BIDDING MADE EASY Edwin B. Kantar 10.00
_____ BRIDGE CONVENTIONS Edwin B. Kantar 7.00
_____ BRIDGE HUMOR Edwin B. Kantar 5.00
_____ COMPETITIVE BIDDING IN MODERN BRIDGE Edgar Kaplan 7.00
_____ DEFENSIVE BRIDGE PLAY COMPLETE Edwin B. Kantar 15.00
_____ GAMESMAN BRIDGE—Play Better with Kantar Edwin B. Kantar 5.00
_____ HOW TO IMPROVE YOUR BRIDGE Alfred Sheinwold 5.00
_____ IMPROVING YOUR BIDDING SKILLS Edwin B. Kantar 4.00
_____ INTRODUCTION TO DECLARER'S PLAY Edwin B. Kantar 5.00
_____ INTRODUCTION TO DEFENDER'S PLAY Edwin B. Kantar 5.00
_____ KANTAR FOR THE DEFENSE Edwin B. Kantar 7.00
_____ KANTAR FOR THE DEFENSE VOLUME 2 Edwin B. Kantar 7.00
_____ SHORT CUT TO WINNING BRIDGE Alfred Sheinwold 3.00
_____ TEST YOUR BRIDGE PLAY Edwin B. Kantar 5.00
_____ VOLUME 2—TEST YOUR BRIDGE PLAY Edwin B. Kantar 5.00
_____ WINNING DECLARER PLAY Dorothy Hayden Truscott 5.00

BUSINESS, STUDY & REFERENCE

_____ CONVERSATION MADE EASY Elliot Russell 4.00
_____ EXAM SECRET Dennis B. Jackson 3.00
_____ FIX-IT BOOK Arthur Symons 2.00
_____ HOW TO DEVELOP A BETTER SPEAKING VOICE M. Hellier 4.00
_____ HOW TO SELF-PUBLISH YOUR BOOK & MAKE IT A BEST SELLER Melvin Powers 10.00
_____ INCREASE YOUR LEARNING POWER Geoffrey A. Dudley 3.00
_____ PRACTICAL GUIDE TO BETTER CONCENTRATION Melvin Powers 3.00
_____ PRACTICAL GUIDE TO PUBLIC SPEAKING Maurice Forley 5.00
_____ 7 DAYS TO FASTER READING William S. Schaill 5.00
_____ SONGWRITERS' RHYMING DICTIONARY Jane Shaw Whitfield 7.00
_____ SPELLING MADE EASY Lester D. Basch & Dr. Milton Finkelstein 3.00
_____ STUDENT'S GUIDE TO BETTER GRADES J. A. Rickard 3.00
_____ TEST YOURSELF—Find Your Hidden Talent Jack Shafer 3.00
_____ YOUR WILL & WHAT TO DO ABOUT IT Attorney Samuel G. Kling 5.00

CALLIGRAPHY

_____ ADVANCED CALLIGRAPHY Katherine Jeffares 7.00
_____ CALLIGRAPHER'S REFERENCE BOOK Anne Leptich & Jacque Evans 7.00
_____ CALLIGRAPHY—The Art of Beautiful Writing Katherine Jeffares 7.00
_____ CALLIGRAPHY FOR FUN & PROFIT Anne Leptich & Jacque Evans 7.00
_____ CALLIGRAPHY MADE EASY Tina Serafini 7.00

CHESS & CHECKERS

_____ BEGINNER'S GUIDE TO WINNING CHESS Fred Reinfeld 5.00
_____ CHESS IN TEN EASY LESSONS Larry Evans 5.00
_____ CHESS MADE EASY Milton L. Hanauer 3.00
_____ CHESS PROBLEMS FOR BEGINNERS edited by Fred Reinfeld 5.00
_____ CHESS SECRETS REVEALED Fred Reinfeld 2.00
_____ CHESS TACTICS FOR BEGINNERS edited by Fred Reinfeld 5.00
_____ CHESS THEORY & PRACTICE Morry & Mitchell 2.00
_____ HOW TO WIN AT CHECKERS Fred Reinfeld 3.00
_____ 1001 BRILLIANT WAYS TO CHECKMATE Fred Reinfeld 5.00

____ 1001 WINNING CHESS SACRIFICES & COMBINATIONS *Fred Reinfeld*	5.00
____ SOVIET CHESS *Edited by R. G. Wade*	3.00

COOKERY & HERBS

____ CULPEPER'S HERBAL REMEDIES *Dr. Nicholas Culpeper*	3.00
____ FAST GOURMET COOKBOOK *Poppy Cannon*	2.50
____ GINSENG The Myth & The Truth *Joseph P. Hou*	3.00
____ HEALING POWER OF HERBS *May Bethel*	4.00
____ HEALING POWER OF NATURAL FOODS *May Bethel*	5.00
____ HERB HANDBOOK *Dawn MacLeod*	3.00
____ HERBS FOR HEALTH—How to Grow & Use Them *Louise Evans Doole*	4.00
____ HOME GARDEN COOKBOOK—Delicious Natural Food Recipes *Ken Kraft*	3.00
____ MEDICAL HERBALIST *edited by Dr. J. R. Yemm*	3.00
____ VEGETABLE GARDENING FOR BEGINNERS *Hugh Wiberg*	2.00
____ VEGETABLES FOR TODAY'S GARDENS *R. Milton Carleton*	2.00
____ VEGETARIAN COOKERY *Janet Walker*	4.00
____ VEGETARIAN COOKING MADE EASY & DELECTABLE *Veronica Vezza*	3.00
____ VEGETARIAN DELIGHTS—A Happy Cookbook for Health *K. R. Mehta*	2.00
____ VEGETARIAN GOURMET COOKBOOK *Joyce McKinnel*	3.00

GAMBLING & POKER

____ ADVANCED POKER STRATEGY & WINNING PLAY *A. D. Livingston*	5.00
____ HOW TO WIN AT DICE GAMES *Skip Frey*	3.00
____ HOW TO WIN AT POKER *Terence Reese & Anthony T. Watkins*	5.00
____ WINNING AT CRAPS *Dr. Lloyd T. Commins*	4.00
____ WINNING AT GIN *Chester Wander & Cy Rice*	3.00
____ WINNING AT POKER—An Expert's Guide *John Archer*	5.00
____ WINNING AT 21—An Expert's Guide *John Archer*	5.00
____ WINNING POKER SYSTEMS *Norman Zadeh*	3.00

HEALTH

____ BEE POLLEN *Lynda Lyngheim & Jack Scagnetti*	3.00
____ DR. LINDNER'S SPECIAL WEIGHT CONTROL METHOD *P. G. Lindner, M.D.*	2.00
____ HELP YOURSELF TO BETTER SIGHT *Margaret Darst Corbett*	3.00
____ HOW YOU CAN STOP SMOKING PERMANENTLY *Ernest Caldwell*	3.00
____ MIND OVER PLATTER *Peter G. Lindner, M.D.*	3.00
____ NATURE'S WAY TO NUTRITION & VIBRANT HEALTH *Robert J. Scrutton*	3.00
____ NEW CARBOHYDRATE DIET COUNTER *Patti Lopez-Pereira*	2.00
____ QUICK & EASY EXERCISES FOR FIGURE BEAUTY *Judy Smith-deal*	2.00
____ REFLEXOLOGY *Dr. Maybelle Segal*	4.00
____ REFLEXOLOGY FOR GOOD HEALTH *Anna Kaye & Don C. Matchan*	5.00
____ 30 DAYS TO BEAUTIFUL LEGS *Dr. Marc Selner*	3.00
____ YOU CAN LEARN TO RELAX *Dr. Samuel Gutwirth*	3.00
____ YOUR ALLERGY—What To Do About It *Allan Knight, M.D.*	3.00

HOBBIES

____ BEACHCOMBING FOR BEGINNERS *Norman Hickin*	2.00
____ BLACKSTONE'S MODERN CARD TRICKS *Harry Blackstone*	3.00
____ BLACKSTONE'S SECRETS OF MAGIC *Harry Blackstone*	3.00
____ COIN COLLECTING FOR BEGINNERS *Burton Hobson & Fred Reinfeld*	5.00
____ ENTERTAINING WITH ESP *Tony 'Doc' Shiels*	2.00
____ 400 FASCINATING MAGIC TRICKS YOU CAN DO *Howard Thurston*	4.00
____ HOW I TURN JUNK INTO FUN AND PROFIT *Sari*	3.00
____ HOW TO WRITE A HIT SONG & SELL IT *Tommy Boyce*	7.00
____ JUGGLING MADE EASY *Rudolf Dittrich*	3.00
____ MAGIC FOR ALL AGES *Walter Gibson*	4.00
____ MAGIC MADE EASY *Byron Wels*	2.00
____ STAMP COLLECTING FOR BEGINNERS *Burton Hobson*	3.00

HORSE PLAYERS' WINNING GUIDES

____ BETTING HORSES TO WIN *Les Conklin*	5.00
____ ELIMINATE THE LOSERS *Bob McKnight*	3.00
____ HOW TO PICK WINNING HORSES *Bob McKnight*	5.00
____ HOW TO WIN AT THE RACES *Sam (The Genius) Lewin*	5.00

___	HOW YOU CAN BEAT THE RACES *Jack Kavanagh*	5.00
___	MAKING MONEY AT THE RACES *David Barr*	5.00
___	PAYDAY AT THE RACES *Les Conklin*	5.00
___	SMART HANDICAPPING MADE EASY *William Bauman*	5.00
___	SUCCESS AT THE HARNESS RACES *Barry Meadow*	5.00
___	WINNING AT THE HARNESS RACES—An Expert's Guide *Nick Cammarano*	5.00

HUMOR

___	HOW TO FLATTEN YOUR TUSH *Coach Marge Reardon*	2.00
___	HOW TO MAKE LOVE TO YOURSELF *Ron Stevens & Joy Grdnic*	3.00
___	JOKE TELLER'S HANDBOOK *Bob Orben*	5.00
___	JOKES FOR ALL OCCASIONS *Al Schock*	5.00
___	2000 NEW LAUGHS FOR SPEAKERS *Bob Orben*	5.00
___	2,500 JOKES TO START 'EM LAUGHING *Bob Orben*	5.00

HYPNOTISM

___	ADVANCED TECHNIQUES OF HYPNOSIS *Melvin Powers*	3.00
___	BRAINWASHING AND THE CULTS *Paul A. Verdier, Ph.D.*	3.00
___	CHILDBIRTH WITH HYPNOSIS *William S. Kroger, M.D.*	5.00
___	HOW TO SOLVE Your Sex Problems with Self-Hypnosis *Frank S. Caprio, M.D.*	5.00
___	HOW TO STOP SMOKING THRU SELF-HYPNOSIS *Leslie M. LeCron*	3.00
___	HOW TO USE AUTO-SUGGESTION EFFECTIVELY *John Duckworth*	3.00
___	HOW YOU CAN BOWL BETTER USING SELF-HYPNOSIS *Jack Heise*	4.00
___	HOW YOU CAN PLAY BETTER GOLF USING SELF-HYPNOSIS *Jack Heise*	3.00
___	HYPNOSIS AND SELF-HYPNOSIS *Bernard Hollander, M.D.*	5.00
___	HYPNOTISM *(Originally published in 1893) Carl Sextus*	5.00
___	HYPNOTISM & PSYCHIC PHENOMENA *Simeon Edmunds*	4.00
___	HYPNOTISM MADE EASY *Dr. Ralph Winn*	3.00
___	HYPNOTISM MADE PRACTICAL *Louis Orton*	5.00
___	HYPNOTISM REVEALED *Melvin Powers*	3.00
___	HYPNOTISM TODAY *Leslie LeCron and Jean Bordeaux, Ph.D.*	5.00
___	MODERN HYPNOSIS *Lesley Kuhn & Salvatore Russo, Ph.D.*	5.00
___	NEW CONCEPTS OF HYPNOSIS *Bernard C. Gindes, M.D.*	7.00
___	NEW SELF-HYPNOSIS *Paul Adams*	7.00
___	POST-HYPNOTIC INSTRUCTIONS—Suggestions for Therapy *Arnold Furst*	5.00
___	PRACTICAL GUIDE TO SELF-HYPNOSIS *Melvin Powers*	3.00
___	PRACTICAL HYPNOTISM *Philip Magonet, M.D.*	3.00
___	SECRETS OF HYPNOTISM *S. J. Van Pelt, M.D.*	5.00
___	SELF-HYPNOSIS A Conditioned-Response Technique *Laurence Sparks*	7.00
___	SELF-HYPNOSIS Its Theory, Technique & Application *Melvin Powers*	3.00
___	THERAPY THROUGH HYPNOSIS *edited by Raphael H. Rhodes*	5.00

JUDAICA

___	SERVICE OF THE HEART *Evelyn Garfiel, Ph.D.*	7.00
___	STORY OF ISRAEL IN COINS *Jean & Maurice Gould*	2.00
___	STORY OF ISRAEL IN STAMPS *Maxim & Gabriel Shamir*	1.00
___	TONGUE OF THE PROPHETS *Robert St. John*	7.00

JUST FOR WOMEN

___	COSMOPOLITAN'S GUIDE TO MARVELOUS MEN Fwd. by *Helen Gurley Brown*	3.00
___	COSMOPOLITAN'S HANG-UP HANDBOOK Foreword by *Helen Gurley Brown*	4.00
___	COSMOPOLITAN'S LOVE BOOK—A Guide to Ecstasy in Bed	7.00
___	COSMOPOLITAN'S NEW ETIQUETTE GUIDE Fwd. by *Helen Gurley Brown*	4.00
___	I AM A COMPLEAT WOMAN *Doris Hagopian & Karen O'Connor Sweeney*	3.00
___	JUST FOR WOMEN—A Guide to the Female Body *Richard E. Sand, M.D.*	5.00
___	NEW APPROACHES TO SEX IN MARRIAGE *John E. Eichenlaub, M.D.*	3.00
___	SEXUALLY ADEQUATE FEMALE *Frank S. Caprio, M.D.*	3.00
___	SEXUALLY FULFILLED WOMAN *Dr. Rachel Copelan*	5.00
___	YOUR FIRST YEAR OF MARRIAGE *Dr. Tom McGinnis*	3.00

MARRIAGE, SEX & PARENTHOOD

___	ABILITY TO LOVE *Dr. Allan Fromme*	7.00
___	GUIDE TO SUCCESSFUL MARRIAGE *Drs. Albert Ellis & Robert Harper*	5.00
___	HOW TO RAISE AN EMOTIONALLY HEALTHY, HAPPY CHILD *A. Ellis*	5.00

_____ SEX WITHOUT GUILT *Albert Ellis, Ph.D.*		5.00
_____ SEXUALLY ADEQUATE MALE *Frank S. Caprio, M.D.*		3.00
_____ SEXUALLY FULFILLED MAN *Dr. Rachel Copelan*		5.00
_____ STAYING IN LOVE *Dr. Norton F. Kristy*		7.00

MELVIN POWERS' MAIL ORDER LIBRARY

_____ HOW TO GET RICH IN MAIL ORDER *Melvin Powers*		20.00
_____ HOW TO WRITE A GOOD ADVERTISEMENT *Victor O. Schwab*		20.00
_____ MAIL ORDER MADE EASY *J. Frank Brumbaugh*		20.00

METAPHYSICS & OCCULT

_____ BOOK OF TALISMANS, AMULETS & ZODIACAL GEMS *William Pavitt*		7.00
_____ CONCENTRATION—A Guide to Mental Mastery *Mouni Sadhu*		5.00
_____ CRITIQUES OF GOD *Edited by Peter Angeles*		7.00
_____ EXTRA-TERRESTRIAL INTELLIGENCE—The First Encounter		6.00
_____ FORTUNE TELLING WITH CARDS *P. Foli*		5.00
_____ HOW TO INTERPRET DREAMS, OMENS & FORTUNE TELLING SIGNS *Gettings*		5.00
_____ HOW TO UNDERSTAND YOUR DREAMS *Geoffrey A. Dudley*		3.00
_____ ILLUSTRATED YOGA *William Zorn*		3.00
_____ IN DAYS OF GREAT PEACE *Mouni Sadhu*		3.00
_____ LSD—THE AGE OF MIND *Bernard Roseman*		2.00
_____ MAGICIAN—His Training and Work *W. E. Butler*		3.00
_____ MEDITATION *Mouni Sadhu*		7.00
_____ MODERN NUMEROLOGY *Morris C. Goodman*		5.00
_____ NUMEROLOGY—ITS FACTS AND SECRETS *Ariel Yvon Taylor*		3.00
_____ NUMEROLOGY MADE EASY *W. Mykian*		5.00
_____ PALMISTRY MADE EASY *Fred Gettings*		5.00
_____ PALMISTRY MADE PRACTICAL *Elizabeth Daniels Squire*		5.00
_____ PALMISTRY SECRETS REVEALED *Henry Frith*		4.00
_____ PROPHECY IN OUR TIME *Martin Ebon*		2.50
_____ SUPERSTITION—Are You Superstitious? *Eric Maple*		2.00
_____ TAROT *Mouni Sadhu*		8.00
_____ TAROT OF THE BOHEMIANS *Papus*		7.00
_____ WAYS TO SELF-REALIZATION *Mouni Sadhu*		3.00
_____ WITCHCRAFT, MAGIC & OCCULTISM—A Fascinating History *W. B. Crow*		7.00
_____ WITCHCRAFT—THE SIXTH SENSE *Justine Glass*		7.00
_____ WORLD OF PSYCHIC RESEARCH *Hereward Carrington*		2.00

SELF-HELP & INSPIRATIONAL

_____ CHARISMA How To Get "That Special Magic" *Marcia Grad*		7.00
_____ DAILY POWER FOR JOYFUL LIVING *Dr. Donald Curtis*		5.00
_____ DYNAMIC THINKING *Melvin Powers*		5.00
_____ GREATEST POWER IN THE UNIVERSE *U. S. Andersen*		5.00
_____ GROW RICH WHILE YOU SLEEP *Ben Sweetland*		7.00
_____ GROWTH THROUGH REASON *Albert Ellis, Ph.D.*		7.00
_____ GUIDE TO PERSONAL HAPPINESS *Albert Ellis, Ph.D. & Irving Becker, Ed. D.*		5.00
_____ HANDWRITING ANALYSIS MADE EASY *John Marley*		5.00
_____ HANDWRITING TELLS *Nadya Olyanova*		7.00
_____ HELPING YOURSELF WITH APPLIED PSYCHOLOGY *R. Henderson*		2.00
_____ HOW TO ATTRACT GOOD LUCK *A. H. Z. Carr*		5.00
_____ HOW TO BE GREAT *Dr. Donald Curtis*		5.00
_____ HOW TO DEVELOP A WINNING PERSONALITY *Martin Panzer*		5.00
_____ HOW TO DEVELOP AN EXCEPTIONAL MEMORY *Young & Gibson*		5.00
_____ HOW TO LIVE WITH A NEUROTIC *Albert Ellis, Ph. D.*		5.00
_____ HOW TO OVERCOME YOUR FEARS *M. P. Leahy, M.D.*		3.00
_____ HOW TO SUCCEED *Brian Adams*		7.00
_____ HUMAN PROBLEMS & HOW TO SOLVE THEM *Dr. Donald Curtis*		5.00
_____ I CAN *Ben Sweetland*		7.00
_____ I WILL *Ben Sweetland*		3.00
_____ LEFT-HANDED PEOPLE *Michael Barsley*		5.00
_____ MAGIC IN YOUR MIND *U. S. Andersen*		7.00
_____ MAGIC OF THINKING BIG *Dr. David J. Schwartz*		3.00

_____ MAGIC OF THINKING SUCCESS *Dr. David J. Schwartz* — 7.00
_____ MAGIC POWER OF YOUR MIND *Walter M. Germain* — 7.00
_____ MENTAL POWER THROUGH SLEEP SUGGESTION *Melvin Powers* — 3.00
_____ NEVER UNDERESTIMATE THE SELLING POWER OF A WOMAN *Dottie Walters* — 7.00
_____ NEW GUIDE TO RATIONAL LIVING *Albert Ellis, Ph.D. & R. Harper, Ph.D.* — 3.00
_____ PROJECT YOU *A Manual of Rational Assertiveness Training Paris & Casey* — 6.00
_____ PSYCHO-CYBERNETICS *Maxwell Maltz, M.D.* — 5.00
_____ PSYCHOLOGY OF HANDWRITING *Nadya Olyanova* — 7.00
_____ SALES CYBERNETICS *Brian Adams* — 7.00
_____ SCIENCE OF MIND IN DAILY LIVING *Dr. Donald Curtis* — 5.00
_____ SECRET OF SECRETS *U. S. Andersen* — 7.00
_____ SECRET POWER OF THE PYRAMIDS *U. S. Andersen* — 7.00
_____ SELF-THERAPY FOR THE STUTTERER *Malcolm Frazer* — 3.00
_____ SUCCESS-CYBERNETICS *U. S. Andersen* — 6.00
_____ 10 DAYS TO A GREAT NEW LIFE *William E. Edwards* — 3.00
_____ THINK AND GROW RICH *Napoleon Hill* — 5.00
_____ THINK YOUR WAY TO SUCCESS *Dr. Lew Losoncy* — 5.00
_____ THREE MAGIC WORDS *U. S. Andersen* — 7.00
_____ TREASURY OF COMFORT *edited by Rabbi Sidney Greenberg* — 5.00
_____ TREASURY OF THE ART OF LIVING *Sidney S. Greenberg* — 5.00
_____ WHAT YOUR HANDWRITING REVEALS *Albert E. Hughes* — 3.00
_____ YOU ARE NOT THE TARGET *Laura Huxley* — 5.00
_____ YOUR SUBCONSCIOUS POWER *Charles M. Simmons* — 7.00
_____ YOUR THOUGHTS CAN CHANGE YOUR LIFE *Dr. Donald Curtis* — 7.00

SPORTS
_____ BICYCLING FOR FUN AND GOOD HEALTH *Kenneth E. Luther* — 2.00
_____ BILLIARDS—Pocket • Carom • Three Cushion *Clive Cottingham, Jr.* — 5.00
_____ CAMPING-OUT 101 Ideas & Activities *Bruno Knobel* — 2.00
_____ COMPLETE GUIDE TO FISHING *Vlad Evanoff* — 2.00
_____ HOW TO IMPROVE YOUR RACQUETBALL *Lubarsky Kaufman & Scagnetti* — 5.00
_____ HOW TO WIN AT POCKET BILLIARDS *Edward D. Knuchell* — 5.00
_____ JOY OF WALKING *Jack Scagnetti* — 3.00
_____ LEARNING & TEACHING SOCCER SKILLS *Eric Worthington* — 3.00
_____ MOTORCYCLING FOR BEGINNERS *I. G. Edmonds* — 3.00
_____ RACQUETBALL FOR WOMEN *Toni Hudson, Jack Scagnetti & Vince Rondone* — 3.00
_____ RACQUETBALL MADE EASY *Steve Lubarsky, Rod Delson & Jack Scagnetti* — 5.00
_____ SECRET OF BOWLING STRIKES *Dawson Taylor* — 5.00
_____ SECRET OF PERFECT PUTTING *Horton Smith & Dawson Taylor* — 5.00
_____ SOCCER—The Game & How to Play It *Gary Rosenthal* — 5.00
_____ STARTING SOCCER *Edward F. Dolan, Jr.* — 3.00

TENNIS LOVERS' LIBRARY
_____ BEGINNER'S GUIDE TO WINNING TENNIS *Helen Hull Jacobs* — 2.00
_____ HOW TO BEAT BETTER TENNIS PLAYERS *Loring Fiske* — 4.00
_____ HOW TO IMPROVE YOUR TENNIS—Style, Strategy & Analysis *C. Wilson* — 2.00
_____ PSYCH YOURSELF TO BETTER TENNIS *Dr. Walter A. Luszki* — 2.00
_____ TENNIS FOR BEGINNERS, *Dr. H. A. Murray* — 2.00
_____ TENNIS MADE EASY *Joel Brecheen* — 4.00
_____ WEEKEND TENNIS—How to Have Fun & Win at the Same Time *Bill Talbert* — 3.00
_____ WINNING WITH PERCENTAGE TENNIS—Smart Strategy *Jack Lowe* — 2.00

WILSHIRE PET LIBRARY
_____ DOG OBEDIENCE TRAINING *Gust Kessopulos* — 5.00
_____ DOG TRAINING MADE EASY & FUN *John W. Kellogg* — 4.00
_____ HOW TO BRING UP YOUR PET DOG *Kurt Unkelbach* — 2.00
_____ HOW TO RAISE & TRAIN YOUR PUPPY *Jeff Griffen* — 5.00

The books listed above can be obtained from your book dealer or directly from
Melvin Powers. When ordering, please remit $1.00 postage for the first book
and 50¢ for each additional book.

Melvin Powers
12015 Sherman Road, No. Hollywood, California 91605

Notes

Notes